Meg Evans
Hand-Stitched Boxes

Meg Evans
Hand-Stitched Boxes

Plastic Canvas ■ Cross Stitch ■ Embroidery ■ Patchwork

David & Charles

For L. G. Evans OBE

Acknowledgements

For all the line drawings and for his patience and skill in an advisory capacity, my thanks to my husband Laurie. For help with the embroidery and in many other ways, my thanks to Hilary Harrison and Pauline Newlands. To my long-time friend and colleague, Nancy Perrin, who is as enthusiastic about boxes as I am, for her never-failing patience in general, and in particular for her contribution to the Christmas napkin box and the two hexagonal boxes , my grateful thanks.

The publishers would like to thank the Singer Sewing Centre, 1 Muswell Hill, London, for the loan of the sewing machines shown on pages 38–39 and 68–69.

Page 2: *A selection of hand-stitched boxes*, (clockwise from top left) *rectangular box with ribbon, cross-stitch sewing box, pincushion box, medium embroidered box and embroidered linen box*

A DAVID & CHARLES BOOK

First published in the UK in 1996
Reprinted 1996, 1997, 1998
First paperback edition 2004

Text and designs copyright © Meg Evans 1996, 2004
Photography and layout copyright © David & Charles 1996, 2004

Distributed in North America
by F&W Publications, Inc.
4700 East Galbraith Road
Cincinnati, OH 45236
1-800-289-0963

Meg Evans has asserted her right to be identified as author of this work in accordance with the Copyright, Designs and Patents Act, 1988.

A catalogue record for this book is available from the British Library.
ISBN 0 7153 1778 4

Photography by Tim Hill
Styling by Zoë Hill
Photography on pages 12-13, 20, 71, 98 and 114 by Paul Biddle
Book design by Margaret Foster

Printed in China by SNP Leefung
for David & Charles
Brunel House   Newton Abbot   Devon

Contents

An Introduction to Box Making

I have always loved boxes: as a small child discarded boxes would be utilised for all those small treasures in which the young delight. Most coveted of all were cigar boxes, made from real wood, and with a wonderful, evocative smell of their former contents.

Still, in adulthood, my enthusiasm remains unabated. Special items, such as cut glass or expensive chocolates are often packaged in very luxurious boxes, well worth keeping for later use. As with other items, which might come in useful later, they take their place in the attic, to be sought out when the need arises.

Then came the discovery that making boxes was not at all difficult. The first box I ever made was embroidered on cotton canvas and lined with card. It was a revelation to me when this floppy, rather messy-looking box shape in embroidery was transformed into a compact, firm little box merely by lining it with card. Having made it by trial and error I knew I could do better next time!

Boxes may be made in a great variety of sizes and shapes – from large and impressive to charmingly small. They may be circular, square, hexagonal or practically any other shape. They may have fit-on, slip-in or fit-over lids, which may also be cut into frames for the inclusion of patchwork or embroidery.

The choice of boxes in this book is excitingly wide, with all the techniques clearly explained and alternatives given to encourage you to make your own boxes. You're sure to find just what you want, and more – whether you need a roomy sewing box, a pretty place to keep your favourite jewellery or a customised box to give as a gift.

The boxes are of three main types – those made from plastic canvas, those from fabric and card and those from a mixture of both. For clarity's sake they have been placed into four groups. Part One shows how to make a wide selection of circular boxes, many with beautiful patchwork tops. Part Two contains a variety of rectangular, square and hexagonal boxes, decorated with generous embroidery or covered with gorgeous padded fabrics. Part Three describes drop-sided boxes, some of which have intriguing gussets, the sides falling open when the lid is removed, and Part Four has a selection of quick but rewarding easy-to-make boxes.

To help you choose which boxes to make each project has been rated to indicate the general level of skill required for its successful completion.

❏ suitable for absolute beginners.

❏ ❏ suitable for beginners but including some charts to read.

❏ ❏ ❏ suitable for those with average sewing ability where a little extra skill is required. Embroidered or patchwork lids to be worked.

❏ ❏ ❏ ❏ suitable for those with moderate ability in sewing, embroidery and patchwork.

❏ ❏ ❏ ❏ ❏ suitable for those with reasonable experience. These are the most intricate projects but are all achievable with a little extra patience and skill.

Opposite: *The choice of boxes is excitingly wide:* (clockwise from top left) *small circular embroidered box, blue print square box, 'memories' box, Christmas napkin box and small patchwork box*

Before You Start

I am sure you long to skip straight to the exciting business of actually making boxes, but please resist just for a little while and read the following section. It contains a wealth of important information which is necessary for the successful completion of the box projects.

MATERIALS

The materials required for each project are given at the beginning of the text. For the sake of clarity the cutting lists are given next, though it might be preferable to cut some of the items later, as the project progresses.

Measurements are given in imperial and metric terms. These may not be exact conversions as amounts are rounded to some extent. Where goods are sold by measurement or weight, the term used by the manufacturer is given, for example, 8m skeins, 2mm card and 9mm ribbon. Fabric lengths are given to the nearest ¼yd/m, except where a very small amount is needed in which case the actual size is given.

Whilst every effort has been made to give accurate measurements and quantities, variations may occur due to different ways of working and project adaptation. It is therefore essential to check all sizes as you go.

PLASTIC AND COTTON CANVAS

PLASTIC CANVAS

Whereas card needs a mini-workshop for successful use – craft knife, cutting board, steel rule, hard pencil, circle cutter – plastic canvas is easier to handle. It may be cut with scissors and may also be used for lining boxes, with the added advantage that the box will be completely washable. These characteristics make it ideal for working on in the evenings, while watching television, or for taking on holiday.

Plastic canvas is available with seven, ten and fourteen bars to the inch, with the 7-count size available in various stiffnesses. It should be cut to the specified size between the bars, counting **bars** not holes. Where edges have been cut, trim off any spikes before starting to stitch, to avoid the yarn catching.

The requirements for plastic canvas are usually given in sheets, though often less is needed. This is because it may need to be cut across the mesh to give the correct length, and half a sheet cut the other way would not do. The cutting list in each project will tell you the exact amount, thus you may use any pieces you have to hand.

The mesh size may vary slightly according to the manufacturer, so if an exact fit is important check the measurements before proceeding. The size of plastic canvas circles may also vary slightly. What are nominally 9½in (240mm) and 6in (152mm) circles, as used in the projects, actually measure 9¼in (235mm) and 5¾in (146mm).

For the sake of clarity and to avoid repetition plastic canvas is referred to as **mesh** in the text at any time when the term 'canvas' might be confused with cotton canvas. The word **canvas** used alone applies to cotton canvas.

COTTON CANVAS

This is available with 10, 12, 14 or 18 threads per inch (25mm). The box on page 53 uses 12 threads per inch (25mm) cotton canvas and in this case it is best to work on an embroidery frame to avoid distorting the canvas.

CARD

Three thicknesses of card are used in the projects. In general the thicker the card, the more stable the box. For the main construction pieces 2mm greyboard is used. Large sheets are available from specialist sources and using this avoids the necessity of joining when making large circular boxes. Greyboard is only pliable along its length, so box sides should always be cut in this direction. 1mm greyboard is used for lining some embroidered and patchwork lids and lining smaller boxes. Thin card is used for some linings, though this need not be bought specially as it is readily available from household packaging. The thickness and quantity of card to be used is specified in each project, though this may be varied. For example, a small circular box could equally well be lined with 1mm card rather than thicker card and lid linings too could be of the thinner card.

CUTTING CARD

This should be done with a Stanley or craft knife, making sure the blade is in good condition. When cutting card for a box side which needs to be moulded remember to cut along the length of card. Mark the line to be cut, place the card on a cutting board and lie the steel rule over the marked section with its edge against the line. This ensures that, should the knife slip, the cut will be made on the spare card rather than on the box section. Begin by making a light incision, holding the handle of the knife as close to the card as possible and vertically against the edge of the ruler, rather than digging the point of the knife into the card. Repeat the cut, putting more pressure on the blade until you have cut right through the card, or to the required depth if you are merely scoring it.

CUTTING CARD CIRCLES

Special tools are available for cutting circles, made by Olfa in two sizes. The smaller one cuts circles between 2in (50mm) and 7⅝in (194mm) diameter and the larger one cuts circles between 2¾in (70mm) and 11¾in (298mm). Another brand, the NT cutter, cuts circles up to 6¾in (170mm) diameter.

If you do not have an Olfa tool, circles may be cut by marking the size required with a compass. Many of the boxes in the book were made this way. First draw a circle of the correct diameter using a hard pencil, applying enough pressure on it to indent the card. Gently score round the line with the craft knife to make a cut. Continue to cut round, gently increasing the pressure on the blade until you have cut right through.

Accuracy is important but when cutting card circles for a box it is more important that they match one another than that they are the exact size specified. Most of my boxes turned out to be slightly different from my original idea. Unless the discrepancy is large there is no need to

re-cut, particularly as the fit is checked at each stage. Sizes of rectangular box linings should be checked against your own box before cutting and any necessary adjustments made.

JOINING CARD

Long lengths of card are needed when making larger circular boxes such as the large embroidered box on page 24 and the hexagonal floral print box on page 64. Though it is always preferable to use card in one piece it is quite satisfactory to join two pieces together using a halving join as described below. For a hexagonal box join the card and then cut the length required. For a circular box make both joins during the construction of the box as described on page 10.

MAKING A HALVING JOIN

Mark a pencil line ½in (13mm) from the edges, and on opposite faces, of the two pieces of card to be joined together. Carefully score along the marked lines through *half the thickness* and cut away the card (fig 1). It may be necessary to rub

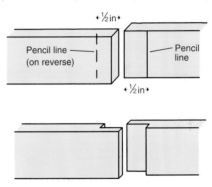

1 Marking and trimming the card to make a join

down the cut away surfaces with an emery board for a smooth and even join. Check that the two pieces of card fit together well before gluing in place (fig 2, page 10). I use clothes pegs to hold joined pieces of card together as the glue dries. Place a small piece of thin card between the peg and the card to prevent indentations. Once the glue has dried, remove the pegs and cut the card to the required length.

For a circular box cut card totalling the length required plus an extra 2in (50mm). The card will need to be dampened. I found that the greyboard I used moulded extremely well without cracking

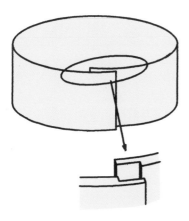

2 Making a halving join

after a few seconds immersion in water. Other types of card may react differently, and it is essential to experiment on scrap card to find what is best for your particular brand.

The dampened side card should be moulded round the base circle, overlapped as necessary, clipped into place and allowed to dry overnight. If the card is moulded round two card circles to form a drum shape a perfect ring will result. On the outside face mark a pencil line against the overlap. Remove the clips and mark a dotted line ½in(13mm) outside this (fig 3). Cut the surplus card away on the dotted line and make a halving join to join the ring.

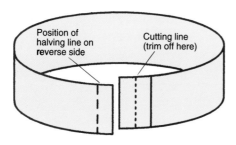

Position of halving line on reverse side

Cutting line (trim off here)

3 Joining a circular box side

For large boxes, if an extra join is necessary, make both joins during the construction of the box, adding an extra 3in (75mm) to the total length. For the box side clip the shorter section outside the larger, mould round the base circle and when dry mark the edges of the long section on the shorter. Remove the clips and mark a dotted line ½in (13mm) outside the marked lines. Cut off the surplus card on these lines and make two halving joins.

When joining the lining, have the shorter length of card inside the longer.

FABRICS

A box is usually covered with one fabric, which may be plain or embroidered, and then lined with a contrasting fabric. If a soft, padded look is required, wadding (batting) is placed between the fabric and the card. If a firm, smooth appearance is preferred, craft Vilene (iron-on interfacing) is used. Lids are usually padded with several layers of wadding to give a rounded appearance. A heavy type of Vilene is used in many of the projects in the book. This craft Vilene is available from specialist suppliers by the yard/metre in a 32in (813mm) width. A narrower width pelmet Vilene is available from furnishing shops.

Cotton is an excellent fabric for box making as it is usually of a firm weave which does not fray and presses well. Polyester cotton is more springy and thus not so easy to press but is still a good choice, especially for linings. To avoid repetition the term cotton is used for both types. Many furnishing fabrics are also ideal and remnants can often be bought at reduced cost. The fabric amounts given in the projects are based on a width of 36in (914mm).

Fabrics used for box making should be selected with care. In general a fine fabric is more suitable for a small box and a medium or heavyweight for a large one. A good quality printed cotton fabric is the easiest to handle. It is firm and the pattern should disguise any small imperfections in workmanship, and it is thus ideal for beginners and the less experienced. Loosely woven fabrics, as used for the embroidered linen box on page 59, are more difficult to handle. If the box top is to be embroidered it is best to plan this first to determine the exact size of the embroidered area and then design the box around this measurement.

Fabrics with a large pattern also need careful planning. For example, a fabric with isolated flowers would look wrong if only half a flower appeared on the top of the box. If the fabric has a 'spot' design this needs to be placed carefully, as in the 'spot' flower print box on page 81. It is helpful to make a window template to assist in cutting the fabric correctly. These may be circular, square or rectangular.

NEEDLES AND YARNS

NEEDLES

For surface embroidery, use a crewel needle, which is sharp with a long eye for easy threading. For canvas and pulled work, use a tapestry needle which has a rounded point. A curved needle is best for stitching up fabric boxes. It does take a little patience to master but gives most satisfactory results.

YARNS

The yarns used and their quantities are specified in each project. The amount given is what was used in each project, but bear in mind that the amount used by individuals can vary. If it seems that you may be running out of a particular yarn, reserve that for the sections where it is important to have the correct colour and substitute one of the other yarns elsewhere, for example, in making up a tray or finishing the inside of a lid.

Paterna stranded wool is a three-strand wool which is easily separated into single strands. To separate the wool and use the number of strands specified hold the end of one strand and gently push the other two down against it to remove them. This single strand may then be used singly or doubled. As plastic canvas is smooth and does not damage the yarn, a length of 36in (1m) may be used in the needle. A shorter length is necessary if working on cotton canvas as there is more wear on the wool as it passes through the canvas.

Anchor stranded cotton has six strands which may be separated as above but extra care is needed to avoid tangles. Never be tempted to separate two strands at once. An alternative method is to cut the length required from the skein, hold it up with the number of strands you wish to separate between the fingers and gently pull apart allowing the thread to twist and separate very gently.

Even when you are using the full six strands in order to get good cover, the strands should be separated and put together again before use.

Anchor Pearl cotton is most readily available in 5gm skeins, occasionally in 10gm balls. If it is important to use this in a long length (as when working edge stitch where it is used up quickly), wind the cotton into a ball. For other uses unwind the skein and cut through the loops opposite the knot which ties the loop together.

The lengths may then be separated from the end with the loop as needed.

RIBBON

Some of the boxes use fine ribbon for **embroidery** and decoration. As you make **a stitch, hold the** ribbon between finger **and thumb and guide it to** keep it flat. **Unthread the needle frequently to** untwist the ribbon.

ADHESIVES

Copydex or a clear adhesive suitable for use with fabric is needed for many of the projects, except in the Easy-to-Make section. Lacing rather than gluing turnings to the back of card is always the best option, as if a mistake has been made this can be rectified. However, gluing can be quite satisfactory and is quicker. Where I have used glue I have indicated this alternative in the text by mentioning gluing before stitching.

CHARTS, STITCH DIAGRAMS AND PROJECT DIAGRAMS

In the charts one square represents one bar or thread of the mesh, canvas or background fabric. The outlines around the designs on the charts to be worked on plastic canvas indicate the cut edge of the mesh. In the stitch diagrams, each line represents a bar or thread. Project and basic technique diagrams are not necessarily to scale.

STITCHING

When stitching on canvas or plastic canvas work each stitch in two movements, bringing the needle up and pulling it through, then taking it down and pulling it through. When working free embroidery on fabric the needle may be taken in and out in one movement. The various stitches used in the projects are described on pages 122 to 126).

BASIC TECHNIQUES

To avoid excessive repetition techniques common to several of the projects are described on pages 104 to 121 and the references to the relevant section are indicated by letters in the projects. A few are not used in the actual projects but are there to provide alternative ways of completing the projects and to help you in designing and making your own boxes.

Circular Boxes

Circular boxes are the simplest form of construction and therefore relatively easy to make. Those in this section are a tempting mixture, ranging from small boxes which are quick and easy, to larger more complex designs which require more time and skill to achieve a polished result. All the boxes are meticulously designed and described in clear steps to make construction easy, which should result in impressive and well-crafted results every time.

The boxes have sides covered with striking fabrics or embroidery on plastic canvas and feature highly decorative lids. The first three boxes have crisply folded patchwork lid inserts using patterned and plain fabrics. Other lids are decorated with richly-coloured but easily-worked embroidery and charming cross-stitch motifs. There are also boxes covered with beautifully printed fabrics, luxuriously padded. For example, two of the boxes are made from Laura Ashley furnishing fabric. So if you make your own curtains or soft furnishings and have scraps of fabric left over, what could be nicer than a matching box?

This stunning collection of circular boxes shows how versatile the craft of box-making can be. Each one is described in detail in the following pages; they are (clockwise from top left) *the large embroidered box, the large patchwork box, the small embroidered box, the medium embroidered box and the 'memories' box*

Large Patchwork Box

□ □ □ □

Fabric-covered plastic canvas has been used for this pretty 9½in (240mm) circular box. The lipped lid is decorated with folded patchwork and fits snugly onto the box. The lid consists of two plastic canvas circles with the patchwork sandwiched between them, embroidered to tone with the fabric, while the fitting is a useful divided tray supported by a lower tray, which can be used for keeping small items tidily.

MATERIALS

Plastic canvas: ultra-stiff 7-count, three sheets 12 x 18in (305 x 457mm); one piece 7-count standard mesh (20 x 121 bars) and four 9½in (240mm) diameter circles

2mm card, 10 x 20in (254 x 508mm)

Thin card, 20 x 24in (508 x 610mm)

Fabrics: ¾yd/m patterned; ¾yd/m plain, dark coloured, toning; ½yd/m plain, medium coloured and ¼yd/m plain, light coloured

2oz wadding, 10 x 30in (257 x 762mm)

Craft Vilene, 4½ x 32in (114 x 813mm)

Anchor Pearl cotton No 5, 5gm skeins – seven dark and two light to tone with fabric

Sewing thread to tone with fabric

PREPARATION

1   Cutting the plastic canvas

When using fabric with a prominent pattern, select the section for the box side and make the box of a suitable depth. In the navy version on page 20, this is 4½in (114mm). The depth may be varied to suit the fabric used – a depth of 3½in (90mm) is average, taking fittings comfortably. If making the box shallower, adjust the depth of the fittings as necessary. For the navy box:

Side: Cut one (30 x 121 bars), one (30 x 75 bars) and two backing strips (30 x 8 bars).

Lining: Cut one (29 x 121 bars) and one (29 x 79 bars).

Lid lip: Cut one (4 x 121 bars) and one (4 x 71 bars).

Fittings: Cut one (36 x 121 bars).

Tray base: Cut two bars off the outer edge of one of the mesh circles.

2   Cutting the card

2mm card: Cut a 9in (230mm) circle for mounting the patchwork, and one for lining the inside base.

Thin card: Cut one 9in (230mm) circle for the box base and one for lining the lid. Cut two 8½in (215mm) circles for both sides of the tray base. Cut two circles just over 5½in (140mm) for the lower tray base. (The edge should be between the two outer bars, allowing room for stitching up.) Keep the remaining card for the tray lining.

3   Cutting the fabric

Patterned fabric: For the side of a 4½in (114mm) deep box, cut one piece 6 x 32in (152 x 813mm). For the outside base and inside lid, cut two circles 9in (230mm) diameter plus an extra ¾in (19mm) all round for turning. For outer and inner base of the lower tray, cut two circles 5½in (140mm) diameter plus ¾in (19mm) extra for turning.

Plain dark fabric: For the side lining of a 4½in (114mm) deep box, cut one piece on the cross in the dark colour 6 x 30in (152 x 762mm). For the inside base and underside of the tray, cut two circles to cover the thin card, allowing ¾in (19mm) extra for turning.

Patchwork: For the backing cut one piece of light plain fabric 9in (230mm) square. For the patches cut seventeen pieces measuring 1¾ x 13in (44 x 330mm) – seven patterned, four dark plain, two medium plain and four light plain.

4   Covering the card circles (see page 104/A)

With the patterned fabric, cover the thin card for the inside lid and the box outer base. With the plain, dark coloured fabric, cover the 2mm card for the inside base and the thin card for both sides of the tray base.

MAKING UP AND LINING THE BOX

For instructions on making and lining the box see pages 106–7/E & F

MAKING THE LID

1   To make the folded patchwork follow the instructions on page 112/K. Mount this onto the 9in (230mm) 2mm card circle (see page 105/C).

The green version of the large patchwork box. The navy and red version is shown on page 20

2   To work the embroidery use the Pearl cotton doubled and work a row of tent stitches in main colour over the bar next to the edge of the two mesh circles. On one of these work a row in contrast colour, followed by another row in main colour, for the lid frame.

See page 106/D for making a fit-on lid with lip.

FITTING THE BOX
1   Cutting the plastic canvas
From the piece of mesh (36 x 121 bars) for the tray side, cut one (9 x 121 bars) and one (9 x 71 bars).

Tray divisions: Cut three (8 x 20 bars).

Pin box side: Cut one (7 x 64 bars) from the standard mesh.

Lower tray: Cut one side (9 x 121 bars), one backing piece (9 x 8 bars) and one division (9 x 39 bars).

Lower tray base: Cut sufficient bars off the outer edge of the circle remaining by cutting the aperture in the lid to leave a circle of nineteen bars radius. Trim off the spikes.

2   To finish your box, see page 111/J for details of making the trays.

Medium Patchwork Box

❑ ❑ ❑

This 6in (152mm) circular box (shown on page 18) is beautifully decorated with a folded patchwork top and side embroidery in tent and long cross stitch in toning yarns. The use of some Pearl cotton gives a wonderful lift to the stitchery. The lid fits over a rising lining and is therefore flush with the sides. The patchwork is mounted onto the lid lining and set in behind the frame while the interior is lined in mixed patterned and plain fabrics.

MATERIALS

Plastic canvas: ultra-stiff 7-count, one sheet 12 x 18in (305 x 457mm); standard or soft 7-count, one piece (6 x 64 bars) for the lower tray side and three 6in (152mm) diameter circles

1mm card, 6in (152mm) square

Thin card, 6 x 24in (152 x 610mm)

Fabrics: ½yd/m patterned; ¼yd/m light plain, and one piece 6 x 10in (152 x 254mm) dark plain

2oz wadding, ¼yd/m

Paterna stranded wool, 8m skeins – five brown 471, three peach 873

Anchor Pearl cotton No 5, 5gm skeins – two light peach 778

Sewing thread to tone with fabrics

PREPARATION

1   Cutting the plastic canvas

Lid side: Cut one (5 x 120 bars).

Backing strip: Cut one (5 x 8 bars).

Box side: Cut one (10 x 120 bars).

Backing strip: Cut one (10 x 8 bars).

Side lining: Cut one (13 x 119 bars).

Tray side: Cut one (6 x 112 bars).

Lower tray side: Cut one (6 x 64 bars). .

Tray dividers: Cut one (6 x 34 bars) and one (6 x 16 bars).

Tray base: Cut two bars off the outer edge of one of the mesh circles.

2   Cutting the card

Cut one 5½in (140mm) circle in 1mm card. Using a mesh circle as a guide, cut two circles in thin card just a little smaller. Cut two circles of thin card a little smaller than the trimmed mesh circle.

3   Cutting the fabric

Patterned fabric: For the box lining, cut one piece on the cross 3½ x 18 in (90 x 457mm). For both sides of the base, underside of the tray and inside lid, cut four circles the size of the card, allowing ¾in (19mm) extra all round for turning.

For the patchwork: For the patches, cut 1¼ x 10in (32 x 254mm) pieces – five light plain, four dark plain and four patterned. For the backing, cut one piece 6in (152mm) square in light plain fabric.

4   Covering the card circles

Cover the 1mm card circle, the two larger thin card circles and one smaller circle for the base of the tray with patterned fabric (see page 104/A).

WORKING THE EMBROIDERY

Use two strands of the Paterna wool and the Pearl cotton doubled.

1   For the box side, tack the mesh backing strip (10 x 8 bars) to the right edge of the side mesh

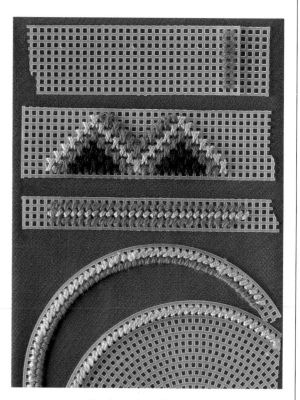

Working the embroidery

(10 x 120 bars), underlapping it by four bars. Leaving the first and last four bars uncovered, work the zigzag line of long cross stitch in Pearl cotton, going up and down seven stitches. On each side of this work a line in light coloured wool, filling in with dark coloured wool (see the photograph on page 16). Lap the left edge over the backing strip to form a ring and tack in place, matching up the four bars. There will be a slight gap between the two edges. Complete the embroidery through both layers.

2   For the lid side, tack the mesh backing strip (5 x 8 bars) to the right edge of the side mesh (5 x 120 bars), underlapping it by four bars. Leaving the first and last four bars uncovered, work three lines of tent stitch in light coloured wool, Pearl cotton and light coloured wool again, then overlap and complete as for the box side.

3   For the lid frame, work a border of tent stitch in Pearl cotton over the bar next to the edge of one full-size mesh circle.

MAKING UP AND LINING THE BOX

1   For making up the box follow the instructions on page 106/E.

2   For lining the box see page 107/F. The lining has been cut to give a 1in (25mm) turning at the top edge to ensure that raw edges will not show above the box side when the lining is in place. Check on this before completing the lacing.

3   For fitting the trays see pages 111/J. In the sample shown on page 18 plain fabric has been used to line the tray.

MAKING THE LID

1   For the patchwork, follow the instructions on page 112/K in the sequence below, placing the patches ½in (13mm) apart.
Centre: four in light plain fabric.
Round 1: alternating patterned and dark plain.
Round 2: alternating dark plain and patterned.
Round 3: light plain.
Round 4: alternating patterned and dark plain.

2   Mount the patchwork onto the 1mm card (see page 105/C) and then follow the instructions for making a lid with a side on page 106/D.

Medium patchwork box lid

Small Patchwork Box

❑ ❑ ❑

The medium patchwork box (left) *and small patchwork box* (above right)

Make the little box, shown opposite, with its smart patchwork lid in fabrics to tone with your bedroom or sitting room, fill it with basic sewing items and you will always have to hand the means of sewing on a missing button or stitching up a faulty hem. Those last-minute panics will be a thing of the past. The lid is made in two sections with the patchwork sandwiched between them with a lipped edge which fits inside the box, holding it in place.

MATERIALS
Plastic canvas: standard 7-count, one sheet
  10½ x 13½in (267 x 343mm) and four 4¼in
  (108mm) diameter circles
1mm card, 4in (102mm) square
Thin card, 12 x 18in (305 x 457mm)
Fabrics: ¼yd/m patterned; ½yd/m plain colour and
  3 x 10in (76 x 254mm) of a second patterned,
  toning fabric
2oz wadding, 10in (254mm) square
Craft Vilene, 2 x 15in (50 x 380mm)
Anchor Pearl cotton No 5, 5gm skeins, three
  dark and one light, to tone with fabric
Sewing thread to tone with fabric

PREPARATION
1   Cutting the plastic canvas
Side: Cut one (14 x 91 bars).
Lining: Cut one (13 x 90 bars).
Lid lip: Cut one (3 x 82 bars).
Tray side: Cut one (5 x 82 bars).
Tray dividers: Cut one (4 x 25 bars) and one
  (4 x 13 bars).
Lower tray: Cut one (5 x 42 bars).
Tray base: Cut two bars off the outer edge of one
of the mesh circles.
2   Cutting the card
Cut one 3⅞in (98mm) diameter circle in 1mm
card for mounting the patchwork.
  Cut two circles in thin card just a little smaller
than the base, and two just a little smaller than
the trimmed mesh circle for the tray base. (The
card edge should be between the two outer bars,
allowing for stitching up.)
  Cut one 3½in (89mm) diameter circle for lining the lid.
3   Cutting the fabric
Patterned fabric: For the side, cut one piece 3½ x
14½in (90 x 370mm); for the outside base, cut

one 4in (102mm) diameter circle plus an extra
¾in (19mm) all round for turning.
Plain fabric: For the side lining, cut one piece on
the cross 3½ x 13½in (90 x 343mm); for the base,
underside of the tray and lid lining, cut three
circles to cover the card, allowing ¾in (19mm)
extra all round for turning.
Patchwork: Cut one patterned strip 1¼ x 10in (32
x 254mm) for the centre, two plain and two patterned strips for the outer rows. For backing the
patchwork, cut one piece 4in (102mm) square.
4   Covering the card circles
Cover three of the thin card circles with the
plain fabric, reserving one for the tray until later
(see page 104/A).

MAKING UP AND LINING THE BOX
1   Overlap the two short edges of the side mesh
by three bars and cross stitch them together to
form a ring (fig 4).
2   For making up and lining the box see pages
106–107/E & F. For fitting the box see page 111/J.

4 Joining the mesh into a ring

MAKING THE LID
1   To make the folded patchwork follow the
instructions on page 112/K, in the sequence
below, placing the patches ½in (13mm) apart.
Centre: four patterned.
Round 1: four plain.
Round 2: eight patterned.
Mount this onto the 1mm card circle (see page
105/C).
2   To work the embroidery on the lid frame,
work a line of tent stitch in light Pearl cotton
over the bar next to the edge of the two full size
mesh circles. On one circle only work a second
row in dark Pearl cotton.
3   To complete the lid, follow the instructions
on page 106/D.

Pincushion Box

❑ ❑ ❑

The gorgeous little box shown below is not only attractive to look at but highly practical. It is sure to be well used by any needleworker as half the interior is fitted with a pincushion and the other half acts as a pin box. It has a pretty patchwork lid mounted onto card and set behind a frame of plastic canvas. The lid side is embroidered in the same colours and stitched to the top, fitting completely over the inner box. The inner box side is embroidered and stitched to the base, set in from the edge so the lid fits snugly over it.

MATERIALS

Plastic canvas: standard 7-count, one sheet 10½ x 13½in (267 x 343mm) and three 4¼in (108mm) diameter circles

1mm card, 5in (127mm) square

Thin card, 5 x 10in (127 x 254mm)

Fabrics: ¼yd/m patterned and one piece plain 3 x 10in (76 x 254mm)

2oz wadding, 10in (254mm) square

Anchor Pearl cotton, 8m skeins – three main colour, one contrast and one cream (colours in sample were blue 921, pink 895 and cream 926)

Sewing thread to tone with fabric

Stuffing, ideally wool scraps and cut ends or wadding

PREPARATION

1   Cutting the plastic canvas

Lid side: Cut one (8 x 91 bars).

Inner box side: Cut one (7 x 86 bars).

Thimble holder: Cut one (6 x 23 bars).

Divider: Cut one (7 x 25 bars).

Lining: Cut one (6 x 36 bars).

Fittings: Cut one mesh circle in half just outside the straight line across the centre of the circle. Trim off the spikes from the half with the straight edge and then trim off one bar from the circular edge. Discard the other half.

Opposite *The large and small patchwork boxes.* Above *The pincushion box*

2 Cutting the card

Cut a circle in 1mm card and two circles in thin card just a little smaller than one of the 4¼in (108mm) mesh circles.

3 Cutting the fabric

Patterned fabric: For the base and inside lid, using the cut card as a guide, cut three circles of fabric allowing ¾in (19mm) extra all round for turning. For backing the patchwork cut one piece of patterned fabric 4¼in (108mm) square.

Patchwork: For the patches, cut three strips of patterned and two strips of plain fabric each 1¼ x 10in (32 x 254mm).

4 Covering the card circles

Cover one thin card circle and the 1mm card circle with fabric (see page 104/A).

MAKING THE LID

1 To make the patchwork see page 112/K. Once completed mount onto the 1mm card circle (see page 105/C).

2 For making up the lid with a side, see page 106/D.

WORKING THE EMBROIDERY

Use the Pearl cotton doubled, and see the picture below for guidance.

1 For the lid side, leaving the first and last three bars of the lid side (8 x 91 bars) uncovered, work a zigzag line of long cross stitch in cream, going up and down five stitches. Fill in the triangles with long cross stitch in main colour below and contrast colour above the line.

NOTE: The lid side is only overlapped by three bars, as this is cut from the sheet mesh which is 91 bars long.

2 Overlap the two short edges matching up the three bars, and complete the embroidery through both layers, so forming a ring (see fig 4, page 19).

3 For the inner side, leaving the first and last four bars uncovered, embroider the inner side (7 x 86 bars) with lines of tent stitch, working one row in main colour, one in cream, one in contrast and completing with three rows in main colour.

4 Overlap the two short edges, matching up the four bars, and complete the embroidery through both layers, so forming a ring.

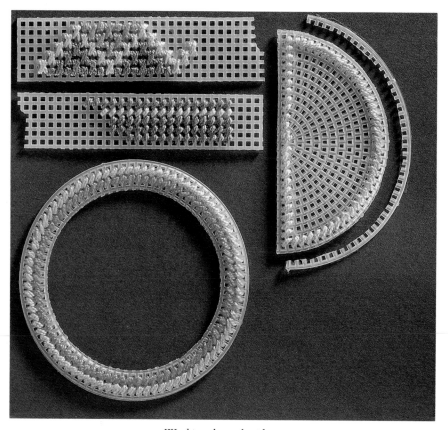

Working the embroidery

5   For the divider, cover the mesh (7 x 25 bars) with tent stitch as above, overcasting each short end as you do so but leaving the long edges uncovered.

6   For the thimble-holder, embroider as for the divider, overcasting all round. Place the two short edges together and overcast to join.

7   For the lid work a line of tent stitch in cream Pearl cotton all round over the bar next to the edge of one mesh circle followed by one in a con-trasting colour. Very carefully cut out the inner uncovered area, taking care to leave one bar inside the embroidery. Trim off the spikes and overcast the inner edge in main colour. Do the same with the prepared mesh half circle, cutting out the centre and overcasting in the same way.

ASSEMBLING THE PIN BOX

1   For the pincushion, cut a piece of fabric very slightly smaller than the prepared half circle and stitch in place behind the opening using toning thread. Trim off any fabric extending beyond the outer edge.

2   Overcast the upper edge of the inner divider (7 x 25 bars) to the straight edge of the prepared half circle. Then overcast the free edge of the divider to the centre bar of a full mesh circle taking the stitches over the straight line of bars across the centre (fig 5a).

3   Overcast the prepared inner box side in place, taking the stitches over the bar next to the edge of the circle.

4   Using toning thread, slip stitch one of the covered circles to the underside of the prepared box base, taking the stitches over every other bar of the mesh (fig 5b).

5   Overcast round the top edge of the inner box side, joining the half circle to the edge. Stuff the pincushion before finishing the stitching.

6   Cut a half circle of card to fit the box area, cover with fabric and slip into place.

7   Position the thimble holder with the joined edges in the corner and slip stitch into place.

8   Edge stitch the outer box side to the prepared lid frame and then edge stitch round the base.

9   Spot glue the edges of the prepared patch-work and place centrally behind the frame. Hold until bonded then slip stitch into place.

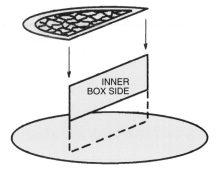

5a Attaching the divider and pin cushion

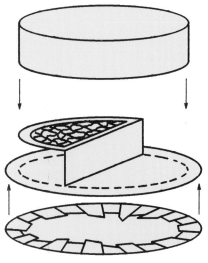

5b Stitching the card to the base

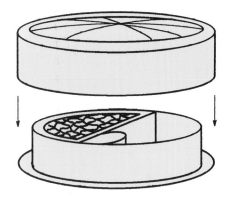

5c The completed pinbox

The interior of my pin box is not lined. If you wish to line yours cut one piece of mesh (6 x 36 bars) and one (6 x 24 bars). Cover with fabric leaving the lower turnings free. Place inside the box and slip stitch round the top edge before lining the base. The base lining will cover the raw edges. When all the glue is dry slip on the lid (fig 5c)

Large Embroidered Box

□ □ □ □ □

The beautiful arabesque stitchery on this 9in (230mm) box (shown on pages 26 and 27) was worked in stranded cotton, from a design taken from a sixteenth-century tile pattern. The box is made of card covered with furnishing fabric, with a slip-in embroidered lid and is fitted with a circular lower tray which may be removed from the box when in use, and an upper tray which rests on this.

The exterior fabric has a fairly coarse weave, the plan being to cut the side fabric on the straight grain, so that the weave ran round the box. This was good from an economical point of view, but possibly not sufficiently stretchy to give a smooth fit. It transpired that the natural 'give' of the fabric was ideal for box making, giving a very smooth finish, even though cut on the straight grain. Always test fabric for stretch before buying. If it is very firm purchase sufficient to cut the side on the cross grain.

The box is lined in a cream furnishing taffeta-type weave fabric, left over from a previous project. There was insufficient to line the whole of the box, so the lower tray was covered with the outer fabric. The measurements given below allow all the lining to be completed in the one fabric.

MATERIALS

2mm card, 20 x 32in (510 x 810mm)
1mm card, 15 x 18in (254 x 380mm)
Thin card, 9 x 18in (380 x 450mm)
Medium to heavyweight furnishing or dress fabric, ½yd/m of 52in (1320mm) width
Light to medium-weight cotton or silk lining fabric, ½yd/m
2oz wadding, ½yd/m
Anchor stranded cotton, 8m skeins – I used one skein each of dark pink 39, mid pink 75, light pink 48, dark green 861, mid green 214, light green 259, mid blue 136, blue 117, mauve 108, coffee 373, light peach 880, cream 885
Sewing thread to tone with fabrics
Tracing paper, 10in (254mm) square
Embroidery transfer pencil
Hoop embroidery frame, 10in (254mm)

PREPARATION

1   Cutting the card for the box
2mm card:
Box side: Cut one piece 3 x 30¼in (76 x 768mm).
Lining side: Cut one piece 2¾ x 30in (70 x 762mm).
Top and base: Cut two circles 9in (230mm) diameter.
Cut one circle 8½in (215mm) diameter for the lid lining and one 8¾in (222mm) for the base lining.

2   Cutting the card for the tray
2mm card:
Upper tray side: Cut one 1⅛ x 28in (28 x 711mm).
Pin box side: Cut one ⅞ x 11in (22 x 280mm).
Tray dividers: Cut three ⅞ x 2⅝in (22 x 66mm).
Lower tray side: Cut one 1 x 21in (25 x 533mm).
1mm card:
Tray base: Cut two circles 8⅛in (206mm) diameter.
Pin box base: Cut two circles 2⅝in (67mm) diameter.
Lower tray base: Cut two circles 5⅝in (143mm) diameter.

3   Cutting the fabric
Outer fabric: For the side, cut one strip 5 x 30½in (127 x 775mm).Using the card as a guide, cut one circle for the base allowing 1in (25mm) extra all round for turning and one 13in (330mm) square for the lid. Overcast the edges of the square to avoid fraying.
Lining: For the sides cut four pieces on the cross, for the box one piece 6 x 27in (152 x 686mm), for the tray one piece 3½ x 26in (90 x 660mm), for the pinbox one piece 3½ x 10in (90 x 254mm), and for the lower tray side one piece 3½ x 18in (90 x 457mm). Using the card circles as a guide, and allowing 1in (25mm) extra all round for turning, cut one base, one inside lid and two each for the trays and pinbox. For the dividers cut three pieces 3½in (90mm) square.

TRANSFERRING THE DESIGN

1   One quarter of the design is shown in the template opposite. To draw the whole design trace around this using a medium pencil.

2 On a large sheet of drawing paper (at least 10in/254mm square) draw a 9in (230mm) square and mark it into quarters. Place the tracing pencilled side down on one quarter, matching up the lines and go round the design using a hard pencil, to transfer the pattern. Go over the design in pencil to give a good outline. Repeat for the other three quarters. Then make a tracing of the completed design using the embroidery transfer pencil.

3 Run a line of tacking to mark the centre in both directions of the square of fabric for the top. Place this right side up with the design, right sides down, over it. Line up the centre lines carefully and pin in place near the edges. Press with a hot iron to transfer the design.

WORKING THE EMBROIDERY

Start at the centre and work outwards, using the photograph on pages 26 and 27 to guide you. Use two strands of cotton for the stem stitch outlines, three strands for the main embroidery and six strands for the French knots. The stem stitch outlines may be worked in the hand but the hoop frame should be used when working the long and short stitch and the French knots. Care should be taken when working without the frame to avoid puckering the fabric.

MAKING AND LINING THE BOX

Select the card for the box side and the circles for the base and top. See pages 109–111/I for making and lining the box, and page 108/G for making the lid.

FITTING THE BOX

A tray is made in the same way as a fabric and card fit-over lid with sides (see page 63).

1 Prepare the sides, bases and base linings for the tray, lower tray and pinbox (see the initial instructions on page 111/J).

2 Stitch the bases to the tray sides and place the lining in the lower tray and pin box.

3 Cover the dividers with fabric as follows. Fold the fabric in half widthways, right sides outside, and press to mark the centre fold line. Place right side down with the card for the divider over it, the top edge against the fold line. Fold over the two side edges against the card and press (fig 6a, page 26). Fold over and press the lower edge over the card (fig 6b). Turn under the remaining edge and fold down to cover the card. The edges should just meet (fig 6c). Adjust if necessary, trim the turnings and slip stitch the three edges.

Template for the embroidery design

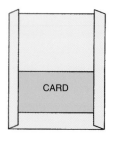

6a Placing the card on the
wrong side of the fabric

6b Folding the turnings
over the card

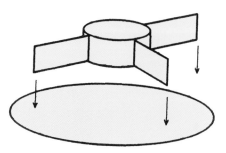

6c Divider ready for slip stitching

6d Attaching dividers to base lining

4   Slip stitch the dividers to the prepared pinbox, two on opposite sides and one halfway between. Try the dividers in the prepared tray to ensure that they are a good fit, adjusting the size if necessary. Run a line of gathering stitch round the edge of the circle of fabric for covering the base. Slip stitch or glue the pinbox and dividers centrally onto it, with the stitched edges at the base (fig 6d). Lie right side down with the remaining card circle over it. Pull up the threads and tie in a bow. Turn to the right side and if necessary ease the fabric so that the dividers are correctly placed. Tie off the ends securely and place in the tray (see page 63). Slip stitch the dividers to the tray edge.

*The large embroidered box and the lid of the
medium embroidered box*

Medium Embroidered Box

A light coloured printed fabric has been used for the top of this pretty 6in (152mm) box, re-embroidered in toning colours to emphasise the flower design. A darker, toning print fabric with a small all-over pattern covers the side. A circle of mesh is embroidered for the frame and the completed embroidery placed behind it. The lid is a fit-on, framed type, the lip fitting snugly inside the box. A 'spot' motif has been used here, but a fabric with an overall design of the right type would also give good results. As an alternative the outline of the design could be quilted instead of re-embroidered.

MATERIALS

Plastic canvas: ultra-stiff 7-count, one sheet 12 x 18in (305 x 457); standard 7-count, one piece (7 x 64 bars) and four circles 6in (152mm) diameter

1mm card, 6 x 12in (152 x 305mm)

Thin card, 6in (152mm) square

Fabrics: ½yd/m patterned with a suitable motif about 5in (127mm) across and ¼yd/m dark fabric with a small print

2oz wadding, 5 x 15in (127 x 380mm)

Craft Vilene, 2¾ x 20in (70 x 508mm)

Anchor Pearl cotton No 5, 5gm skeins – four dark and one light

Anchor stranded cotton, 8m skeins – one skein each of suitable colours, to complement the fabric

Sewing thread to tone with the lining

Hoop embroidery frame, 6in (152mm)

PREPARATION

1   Cutting the plastic canvas

Side: Cut one (15 x 121 bars).

Backing strip: Cut one (15 x 8 bars).

Lid lip: Cut one (3 x 112 bars).

Box lining: Cut one (14 x 120 bars).

Lower pin box: Cut one (6 x 64 bars).

Tray side: Cut one (6 x 112 bars).

Dividers: Cut one (6 x 34 bars), one (6 x 16 bars).

Tray base: Cut two bars off the outer edge of one of the mesh circles.

Lower tray: Cut one (7 x 64 bars).

2   Cutting the card

1mm card:

For mounting the embroidery: Cut one 5⅛in (130mm) diameter circle.

Thin card:

Lining for both sides of the base: Cut two circles just a little smaller than a mesh circle.

Using the trimmed circle as a guide, cut two circles just a little smaller.

Cut one circle 5¼in (133mm) for lining the lid.

3   Cutting the fabric

Patterned fabric:

In order to work the correct amount of embroidery for the top it is helpful to cut out the aperture from the mesh circle for the lid before starting work and use this as a guide. Place over the pattern on the fabric to decide exactly which section is to be embroidered and cut out a square at least 1½in (38mm) bigger all round.

Side lining: Cut one piece on the cross 3¼ x 18in (82 x 457mm).

Lining the lid, base and underside of the tray: Use a card circle as a guide and cut four circles of fabric, allowing ¾in (19mm) extra all round for turning.

Dark fabric: For the side, cut one piece 3½ x 19½in (89 x 496mm) and one circle ¾in (19mm) larger than the card for the outer base.

4   Covering the card circles

With the patterned fabric cover one circles for the base, one for the tray and one for the lid lining. (See page 104/A.)

WORKING THE EMBROIDERY

1   Begin by marking the size of the aperture onto the fabric with a line of tacking. Then using two strands of cotton for the embroidery, follow the printed design in a mixture of stem stitch, long and short stitch and French knots (see the photograph opposite for guidance). Outline the flowers and leaves in stem stitch, holding the fabric in the hand.

2   Mount the fabric onto a hoop frame before filling in with long and short stitches, and French knots at the centre of the flowers. The outline should be omitted on small shapes. Some spaces may be left uncovered, as this gives added depth to the embroidery.

If you prefer to complete all the embroidery in the hand take care to keep the work flat and not pull the stitches across the back.

MAKING UP AND LINING THE BOX

See pages 106–7/E and F.

MAKING THE LID

1   Work a border of tent stitch in contrast Pearl cotton over the bar next to the edge of the two mesh circles (see page 106/D) then prepare and mount the embroidery as shown on pages 104–5/B.

2   See page 106/D for instructions on making a fit-on lid with lip.

FITTING THE BOX

To complete your box, fit it following the instructions on page 111/J.

Small Embroidered Box

□ □ □ □

Any new home owner would be delighted to receive a house-warming gift in the form of a box made from furnishing fabric used in their sitting room or bedroom. This 4½in (114mm) box (pictured on page 13) is made of fabric and card with a fit-on framed lid. The fabric used is dupion, a type of textured rayon, while the embroidery is worked on a loosely woven voile. Linen scrim, such as the dish-cloth used in the box on page 59, could be substituted, or any other lightweight fabric of loose weave.

The design inspiration was a greetings card showing a detail of Van Gogh's painting Flowers in a Vase, though you can find ideas from any source, such as the photograph shown below. Fifteen different colours of stranded cotton were used, all from my 'bits' box – an ideal way to use up hoarded threads. Select dark, medium and light colours which tone with your fabric. The pattern is worked freely, using six strands of stranded cotton to give a rich, raised surface. As an alternative to the free embroidery, cross stitch on Aida, tent stitch on cotton canvas or surface stitchery on the fabric itself could be used.

MATERIALS

2mm card, 13 x 15in (330 x 380mm)

Thin card, 5in (125mm) square

Lightweight furnishing dupion or similar fabric for the box, 10 x 15in (250 x 380mm)

Furnishing voile or similar fabric for the embroidery, 6in (150mm) square

Dupion or other lightweight fabric such as cotton or silk for the lining, ½yd/m

2oz wadding, 8 x 15in (203 x 380mm)

Anchor stranded cotton, a selection of colours

Sewing thread to tone with fabrics

Hoop embroidery frame, 4in (102mm)

PREPARATION

1   Cutting the card

2mm card:

Base: Cut two circles 4in (102mm) in diameter.

Lid: Cut two circles, one 4⅜in (112mm) and one 4in (102mm) in diameter.

Side: Cut one piece 2 x 14in (50 x 356mm).

Lining: Cut one piece 1⅞ x 13in (22 x 330mm).

Designing the embroidery

Thin card:
To mount the embroidery: Cut one circle 3¾ (95mm) in diameter.

2 Cutting the fabric

Box lid and base: Using the card circles as a guide and allowing ¾in (19mm) extra all round for turning, cut two circles in dupion and two in lining fabric.

Box side: Cut one piece in dupion 3½ x 14in (90 x 356mm).

Box side lining: Cut one piece in the lining fabric 3 x 13in (76 x 330mm) on the cross grain.

WORKING THE EMBROIDERY AND MAKING THE LID

1 Place the larger card for the lid over the centre of the voile and using a hard pencil or water-erasable marker draw all round it. Draw a second line inside this to mark the area to be embroidered.

2 Place the voile in the hoop frame. No pattern is needed as the stitches are worked freely by eye, either like the sample shown opposite or from a colourful flower picture of your own. Using the full six strands of cotton, work the flowers and leaves in mixed straight stitch, radiating straight stitch and French knots. Completely cover the background, taking the stitchery slightly over the marked circle to hide the marked line.

3 There is no need to press this type of embroidery. Mount it over card and make up the frame and complete the lid as described on pages 104–5/B and page 108/H.

MAKING UP AND LINING THE BOX
See pages 109–111/I.

Golden Wedding Box
❑ ❑ ❑ ❑

A special occasion such as a golden wedding anniversary deserves a special present. Most couples by this stage have most of the worldly goods they need, so it is often difficult to decide on a suitable gift. What could be better than a hand-made box (shown on page 33) with a wedding photograph, to bring back memories of a happy day, set into the base? A second picture could be added to the inside of the lid.

This box is made of fabric and card with a stunning patchwork top set into a fit-on framed lid. The box side is covered with Aida band, which has a pretty gold edging with wide ribbon stitched onto it. The Aida band is also used in the folded patchwork together with three types of gold ribbon which give a very rich effect. The gold fabric I used was lustrous and difficult to handle. Thus, less experienced needle-workers need to choose the fabric carefully. An alternative could be a pretty gold-coloured cotton fabric. The colours, too, could be changed for celebrating a silver or ruby wedding. If preferred the ribbon could be omitted and the initials of the couple could be worked in cross stitch on the band for the side. Similarly the lid could be embroidered in cross stitch as an alternative to patchwork.

MATERIALS
2mm card, 16 x 20in (406 x 508mm)
1mm card, 6 x 12in (152 x 305mm)
Thin card, 6in (152mm) square
Gold fabric for lid frame and lining, ½yd/m of 36in (914mm) width
Lightweight cream cotton for lining lid and base, 16in (406mm) square
Craft Vilene, ¼yd/m
Aida band, 2in (50mm) wide, 1¼yd/m
Offray ribbon, 39mm wide – ½yd/m of bright gold 5721, ¾yd/m dark gold 3201 and 2yd/m light gold 3201
2oz wadding, ¼yd/m
Sewing thread to tone with gold fabric
2 photographs, size to suit a 4½in (114mm) aperture
Clear acetate (to protect photos, optional), one sheet 5 x 10in (127 x 254mm)

PREPARATION
1 Cutting the card
2mm card:
Lid: Cut two circles 6⅛in (155mm) diameter.

Lid lining: Cut two circles 5¼in (133mm) diameter.

Base: Cut one circle 5⅞in (149mm) diameter.

Side: Cut one 2 x 20in (50 x 508mm).

Side lining: Cut one 1½ x 20in (38 x 508mm).

1mm card:

Base lining: Cut two circles 5⅞in (149mm) in diameter.

Thin card:

For mounting embroidery: Cut one circle 5¼in (133mm) in diameter.

2   Cutting the fabric

Gold fabric:

Lid: Cut two circles using the lid card as a guide, and allowing 1in (25mm) extra fabric all round for turning.

Outer box and interior lining: Cut two lengths on the cross 3 x 20in (76 x 508mm).

Cream fabric:

Using the base lining card as a guide cut two circles, allowing ¾in (19mm) extra for turning. These are for framing the photographs.

For backing the patchwork, cut one piece 6in (152mm) square.

3   Cutting the Vilene

For the side, cut one 2 x 22in (50 x 560mm) and one 1¾ x 20in (44 x 508mm).

4   Cutting the Aida band and ribbon

Aida band: For the outer box, cut one piece 21in (533mm) long, and for the patchwork cut eight pieces 3¼in (82mm) long.

Ribbon: For the outer side cut one piece 21in (533mm) long from the light gold, and for the patchwork cut sixteen pieces 3¼in (82mm) long. From the dark gold cut eight pieces 3¼in (82mm) long. From the bright gold cut four pieces 3¼in (82mm) long.

MAKING UP AND LINING THE BOX

1   See pages 109–111/I for making up and lining.

2   Cover the box side with gold fabric. Make a seam in the Aida band with a long machine stitch or strong hand tacking. Try it over the prepared box side – it should be a tight fit. Adjust the seam if necessary then machine or hand stitch securely. Trim the turnings and overcast the edges to prevent fraying, catching in the edge of the turnings so they will be invisible. Place back over the prepared side. Repeat with the ribbon (fig 7).

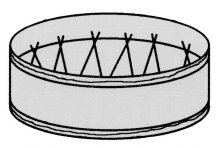

7 Fabric covered side with Aida band

MOUNTING THE BASE PHOTOGRAPH

1   Check that the two circles of card for the base lining are the correct size. Compare the photograph for the base with the card circle (5⅝in/143mm) and decide how wide the frame needs to be. Cut out the centre of one circle to give a frame of the correct width.

2   Make up the base as for a lid with an aperture (see page 108/H). If you do not wish to use photographs put the two card circles together and cover in the usual way.

MAKING THE LID

1   To make the patchwork see page 112/K. The ribbon is prepared in a similar way to fabric. As both edges are finished there is no need to turn over and press one edge. I found it necessary to stitch down the points of the bright gold ribbon because of its springiness.

Centre: four bright gold.

Round 1: eight Aida band.

Round 2: eight dark gold.

Round 3: sixteen light gold.

Mount the patchwork onto the thin card circle.

2   Measure the outer dimension of the box and check that the two card circles 6⅛in (155mm) are the correct diameter. Adjust as necessary. Cut a circle from the centre of one of them leaving a frame ⅝in (16mm) wide. Cover the frame and mount the patchwork behind it (see page 108/H, steps 1 to 6).

3   Check that the two circles of 5¼in (133mm) for the lid lining will slip easily into the box, allowing for their covering of fabric. Frame the photograph in the lid lining as given for the base.

4   Slip stitch or glue to the back of the prepared patchwork lid and your box is complete.

The golden wedding box

'Memories' Box

□ □ □ □

A box lined with a special fabric makes a particularly memorable gift. Every time it is opened it serves as a reminder of an event or a loved one. Having made many clothes in the past my 'bits' bag is full of scraps which bring back memories of times and places – scraps of fabric from a shirt for my first grandchild (now a bearded six-footer), a tiny print from a grand-daughter's dress, worn as a toddler in the Sudan, bringing back memories of a very special family re-union. This box would be a lasting reminder of a wedding day if it was made with a piece of the same fabric used for the bridesmaids' or mother of the bride's dresses, and filled with a gift from the bridegroom.

The cross stitch pattern was adapted from the fabric design and the colours chosen to match. I had very little of my special fabric for the lining, so the lid lining needed to be pieced. I took advantage of this fact and made the centre from linen on which the names of the bride and groom were embroidered. This was cut into a rectangle and strips of fabric stitched to it. A circle was then cut from the joined piece.

Another alternative would be to cover the outer box in this fabric and use a suitably toning fabric for the lining, with no embroidery at all.

MATERIALS

Linen fabric (or similar), 18 threads per 1in (25mm), 10 x 18in (254 x 457mm)
Lightweight silk or cotton lining fabric, 10 x 21in (254 x 533mm)
2mm card, 7 x 20in (178 x 508mm)
1mm card, 1½ x 14in (38 x 356mm)
Anchor stranded cotton, 8m skeins – I used one each of pink 896, peach 9575, brown 905, green 876, mauve 118 and olive 854
2oz wadding, ¼yd/m
Sewing thread to tone with lining fabric
Squared paper

PREPARATION

1   Cutting the card

The dimensions of your box will depend on the the length of the embroidery you work for the box sides. It is therefore advisable to complete the stitching before you cut the card for the box (see instructions for making up and lining the box, on page 35).

2   Cutting the fabric

Linen:
Top: Cut one piece 7in (178mm) square.
Side: Cut one piece 3 x 18in (76 x 457mm).
If embroidering the lid lining, cut one piece 5in (127mm) square.

Special lining:
Base: Cut two circles 6in (152mm) in diameter.
Side: Cut one piece 2½ x 16in (64 x 406mm).
Lid: Cut four strips 2 x 4in (50 x 114mm).
If you do not wish to embroider the lid lining, cut a third circle 6in (152mm) in diameter.

WORKING THE EMBROIDERY

Using the full six strands of cotton and taking the cross stitch over two threads, work a top and side following the charts on page 36. You will need to repeat the pattern for the side (see below).

Linen made by different manufacturers will vary slightly in count so the embroidery for the lid should be worked first in order to estimate the length needed for the side. In the box I worked the embroidery measured 4in (102mm) one way and 4⅛in (105mm) the other. I worked on the 4in (102mm) measurement as this was simpler.

The size of the card for the lid needs to be the width of the embroidery plus at least ⅜in (10mm), allowing for a border all round. To give the right measurement the fabric for the side needs to measure approximately 3½ times the embroidery diameter. Therefore a 14in (356mm) length was needed. Twenty-three repeats of the pattern gave the right length.

1   Work the embroidery for the top and then measure the width.

2   Multiply this measurement by 3½, this is the length required for the side embroidery.

3   Work the number of pattern repeats to give the correct length or just over, as all the patterns must be complete. Join the seam securely by hand or machine.

The 'memories' box (the top of the lid is shown on page 12)

MAKING UP AND LINING THE BOX

See pages 109–111/I for full details for making and lining a box.

1   Cut two 4⅛in (105mm) diameter circles from the 2mm card

Cut 2mm card for the side 1½in (38mm) wide by the length of the embroidery plus 1in (25mm). Dampen it and mould it round the card circles and allow the dry.

2   Place the card inside the embroidery, pressing it out to give a good fit, and mark the position for the halving join. When dry, remove it and make the join (see page 10).

3   Measure the size of the interior of the box and cut a new base and base lining to this size, if different. Cover both with the special lining fabric, see page 104/A. Ladder stitch one circle to the box side and slip the other inside the box.

4   Line the 1mm card for the side lining and place inside the box.

MAKING THE LID

1   Measure the diameter of the completed box from the outside edges and cut a circle of card slightly smaller than this diameter (4⅜in/112mm in the example), to allow for the thickness of the fabric. Using this as a guide cut the embroidery into a circular shape, allowing at least 1in (25mm) all round for turning. Overcast the edge to avoid fraying.

2   Mount the embroidery over the card (see page 108/G).

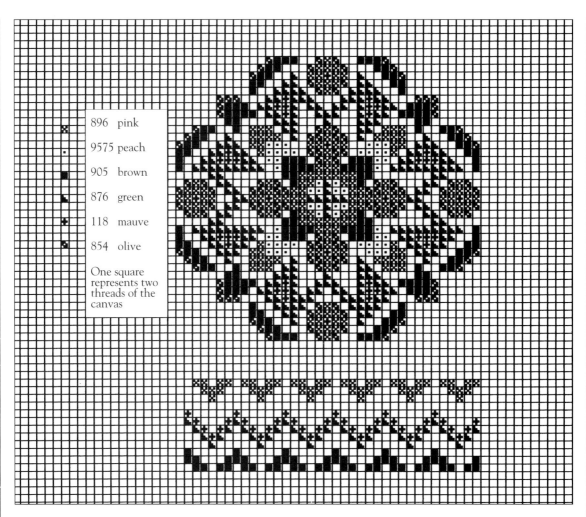

896	pink
9575	peach
905	brown
876	green
118	mauve
854	olive

One square represents two threads of the canvas

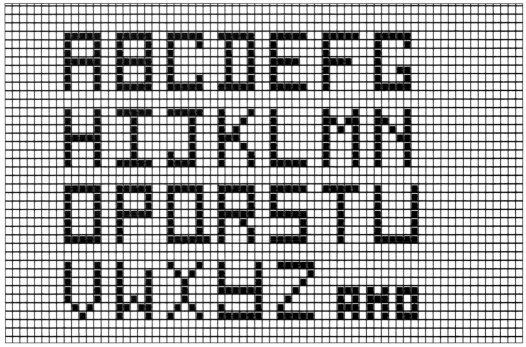

3 Cut out a circle of card ½in (13mm) smaller than the outer lid (3⅞in/98mm in the sample). If you do not wish to embroider the inside lid, cover it with fabric in the usual way (see page 104/A), having first checked that it will slip in and out of the box easily.

COMPLETING THE LID LINING

1 To complete the lid lining with the names of the bride and groom or other wording, first sketch out on squared paper the words or letters needed, using the alphabet charted opposite. As names vary in length you may need to alter the width of letters and the spacing, or use only the initials. The lettering could be worked over just one thread, to leave room for the addition of a date.

2 Mark the centre lines of the material (the 5in/127mm square of linen) with tacking in both directions.

3 Work the names over centre of the fabric in cross stitch. Use this to line the lid, or if setting into lining fabric, continue as follows (fig 8a).

4 Mark a square of tacking for the stitching line two threads outside the lettering. Trim the surplus fabric leaving ⅜in (10mm) outside the tacking (fig 8a). Hand overcast the edges to prevent fraying.

5 Cut four strips of fabric 2 x 4in (50 x 102mm). Place one strip over the lettering panel, right sides facing and stitching lines matched up. Stitch from the linen side exactly along the line of tacking which follows the grain. Place another piece of fabric along the opposite side, stitching lines matched up, and stitch into place (fig 8b). Press, the turnings towards the outer edge then repeat for the other two sides to complete the joining and press again (fig 8c).

6 Cut a square of Vilene to the measurement of the linen panel. Slip stitch or herringbone it to the back, taking the stitches through the machining (fig 8d). Using a card circle as a guide cut this into a circular shape allowing ¾in (19mm) all round for turning. Mount over the card circle for the lid lining, lacing the turnings on the back rather than gluing as this will allow some movement of the fabric to ensure that the embroidered panel is central and straight. Check that it will slip in and out of the box easily. Stitch or glue to the back of the prepared embroidered lid section.

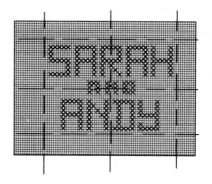

8a Marking out the embroidery

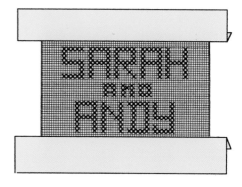

8b Stitching on the fabric strips

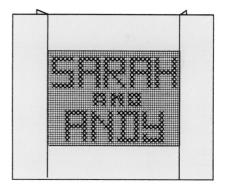

8c Pressing the strips

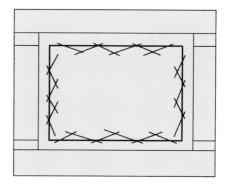

8d Stitching the Vilene in position

Rectangular, Square & Hexagonal Boxes

*F*lat-sided boxes take a little longer to make than circular ones but have an advantage in that they can be made in a wonderful variety of shapes and sizes to suit the shape of the items to be stored. The many fabrics used for the following boxes range from a striped design, used to create a special pattern on the lid of a hexagonal box, to a linen dish cloth, ideal for pulled work embroidery. Some of the boxes are embellished by decorative ribbon, others are edged with embroidery and have tasselled lids. There is even a box in a Christmas print to keep table napkins for the festive season.

The boxes not only vary in shape and covering fabric but also in the time and expertise needed to make them. The simplest is the small square fabric box which is covered in pretty, gold-highlighted fabric. At the other extreme is the embroidered rectangular canvas box which takes extra time and skill to make.

The dimensions of these handsome flat-sided boxes can be altered to suit their intended contents. They are (clockwise from top left): *the embroidered rectangular canvas box, hexagonal floral-print box, rectangular box with ribbon, medium Rhodes stitch box, and* (centre) *the embroidered linen box*

Rectangular Box with Ribbon

❑❑

This is the first of three boxes of similar construction which are relatively quick to make. Card is covered with wadding and then with fabric, which in this box is a dress or patchwork-weight printed cotton. The covered card is then stitched to mesh, which has a decorative embroidered edge to give a pleasing contrast in texture and colour. This box measures approximately 6 x 9in (152 x 230mm) and has a fit-on lid with internal lip. It contains an embroidered tray, which is supported on covered-card tray carriers. However, you may prefer to support the tray on small boxes, as described on page 117/Q.

MATERIALS

Plastic canvas: ultra-stiff, 7-count, two sheets 12 x 18in (305 x 457mm)
2mm card, 14 x 18in (356 x 457mm)
Thin card, 18 x 20in (457 x 508mm)
Fabrics: ½yd/m patterned, ½yd/m contrast, and 3 x 4in (76 x 102mm) Aida or flannel for 'page' of needlecase
2oz wadding, ¼yd/m
Anchor Pearl cotton, 5gm skeins – eight main colour to tone with patterned fabric and four to contrast (in the pink version, pink 895 and cream 926 were used and in the brown version, pink 896 and honey 942)
Sewing thread to tone with patterned fabric
9mm ribbon, ¾yd/m, to tone with fabrics

PREPARATION

1 Cutting the plastic canvas

Base and top: Cut three (62 x 42 bars).
Sides: Cut two (18 x 62 bars) and two (18 x 42 bars).
Lid lips: Cut two (3 x 58 bars) and two (3 x 38 bars).
Tray base, cut one (38 x 58 bars).
Tray sides: Cut two (7 x 58 bars) and two (7 x 38 bars).
Tray dividers: Cut two (6 x 37 bars) and two (6 x 18 bars).
Needlecase: See page 119/S

If you wish to make boxes to support the tray instead of the card supports you will also need six (7 x 38 bars) and four (7 x 7 bars) square.

2 Cutting the card

2mm card:
Box base lining: Cut one 5¾ x 8⅞in (146 x 225mm).
Box side linings: Cut two 2⅜ x 9in (60 x 230mm) and two pieces 2⅜ x 5⅞in (60 x 150mm).
Tray supports: Cut four 1 x 5¾in (25 x 146mm).
Thin card:
Box lid: Cut one 6 x 8¾in (152 x 222mm).
Box outer base: Cut one 5⅞ x 8⅞in (150 x 225mm).
Box sides: Cut two 2 x 8¾in (50 x 222mm) and two 2 x 5¾in (50 x 146mm).
Lid lining and outer base of tray: Cut two 5½ x 8⅜in (140 x 213mm).
Tray divisions: Cut two 1⅞ x 2⅝in (47 x 67mm), one 1¾ x 5½in (44 x 140mm), one 3⅞ x 5½in (98 x 140mm), and one 1⅝ x 2⅝in (41 x 67mm).
Needlecase: See page 119/S.

3 Cutting the fabric and wadding

Patterned: Using the relevant pieces which have been cut from the thin card as a guide and allowing ⅝in (16mm) extra all round for turnings, cut fabric to cover the four side sections, the outer base and the lid.
Contrast: Using the relevant pieces of cut card as a guide and allowing ⅝in (16mm) extra all round for turnings, cut fabric to cover the four side linings, the base lining, the lid lining the underside of the tray, the tray divisions and two pieces for the tray supports.
Wadding: Using the cut thin card as a guide cut four side pieces exactly the size of the card. Using the lid card, the 6 x 8¾in (222 x 152mm) piece, cut three pieces of wadding, one about ¼in (6mm) smaller all round than the card and two more in slightly decreasing size.

PREPARING THE SIDES

1   Using doubled-up Pearl cotton, work a line of tent stitch in contrast colour all round over the bar next to the edge of the two lid pieces and the four sides (see the photograph above). Work a line of tent stitch in main colour lengthways along the centre bar of the four lid lip sections. Cover the thin card for the sides with fabric and wadding (see page 114/L).

2   Slip stitch the covered card to the prepared canvas using matching sewing thread. Repeat for the base, this time omitting the wadding.

MAKING UP AND LINING THE BOX

Stitch up and line the box as described on page 116/O and pages 116–117/P.

MAKING THE LID

To make the lid follow the instructions on page 115/M.

MAKING THE FITTINGS

To finish your box, make the tray by following the instructions on pages 117–118/Q. To make the needlecase see page 119/S

Large Fabric Sewing Box

❑ ❑ ❑

This smart box measures 8½ x 12 x 3in (215 x 305 x 76mm) deep and is made in the same way as the rectangular box with ribbon described in the previous project, with an extra row of tent stitch around the fit-on lid, which picks up a contrasting colour in the fabric. Elsewhere cream is used as the main contrast. The tray rests on two narrow containers which are useful for holding pens and pencils or skeins of thread. The upper tray has a built in pin tray and pincushion and a matching needlecase completes the fittings. For the sake of economy wool has been used to embroider the underlid, the tray and the tray supports.

MATERIALS

Plastic canvas: ultra-stiff 7-count, three sheets 12 x 18in (305 x 457mm)

2mm card, 16 x 24in (406 x 610mm)

1mm card, 8 x 12in (203 x 305mm)

Thin card, 30in (762mm) square

Fabrics: ½yd/m printed fabric, ½yd/m plain and 3 x 4in (76 x 102mm) Aida or flannel for 'page' of needlecase

2oz wadding, 20 x 24in (508 x 610mm)

Paterna stranded wool, 8m skeins – seven main colour 900

Anchor Pearl cotton No 5, 5gm skeins – five main colour 22, two cream 926, one contrast 261

Sewing thread to tone with patterned fabric

PREPARATION

1   Cutting the plastic canvas

Lid, underlid and base: Cut three (55 x 81 bars).

Sides: Cut two (21 x 81 bars) and two (21 x 55 bars).

Lid lips: Cut two (4 x 77 bars) and two (4 x 51 bars).

Tray base: Cut one (51 x 77) bars

Tray side: Cut two (7 x 77 bars) and two (7 x 51 bars).

Tray dividers: Cut two (6 x 50 bars), two (6 x 27 bars) and one (6 x 44 bars).

Pin box/pincushion frame: Cut one (25 x 27 bars).

Tray support boxes: Cut two (51 x 10 bars), four (51 x 8 bars) and four (10 x 8 bars).

Needlecase: See page 119/S

2   Cutting the card

2mm card:

Box side lining: Cut two 2⅞ x 12in (73 x 305mm) and two pieces 2⅞ x 7¾in (73 x 197mm).

Base lining: Cut one 7¾ x 11⅝in (197 x 295mm).

1mm card:

Outer lid: Cut one 7⅜ x 11¼in (188 x 285mm).

Thin card:

Sides: Cut two 2⅜ x 11½in (60 x 292mm).

Outside base: Cut one 7¾ x 11¾in (196 x 298mm).

Lid lining and tray base: Cut two 7⅜ x 11¼in (186 x 285mm).

Tray divisions: Cut one 1⅞ x 7½in (47 x 190mm), one 2⅜ x 7½in (60 x 190mm), one 3½ x 6¾in (90 x 171mm) and one 3⅛ x 3⅞in (79 x 98mm).

Needlecase: See page 119/S.

3   Cutting the fabric and wadding

Using the relevant pieces of cut card as guides cut out the following fabric pieces allowing ⅝in (16mm) extra all round for turnings.

Patterned fabric: Cut four sides, four side linings, one base, one lid and two needlecase covers.

Plain fabric: Cut one inner base, one tray base, one lid lining and two needlecase linings.

Wadding: Cut four sides and one lid lining, using the relevant pieces of cut card as guides. For the lid, cut three pieces, one about ¼in (6mm) smaller all round than the 1mm card and two more in slightly decreasing size.

PREPARING THE SIDES AND FITTINGS

Use the Pearl cotton doubled or two strands of wool, and follow the photograph opposite.

1   For the lid, work a line of tent stitch in cream Pearl cotton followed by one in contrast, starting over the bar next to the edge.

2   For the sides, work a line in cream.

3   For the underlid, work a line in wool.

4   For the lid lips, work a line of satin stitch in wool over two bars along the four lid lip sections.

5   For the tray supports, work lines of satin stitch in wool over two bars to cover the ten sections.

6   For the tray, cover the sides and dividers with satin stitch.

7 For the pin box frame, work a rectangle of tent stitch all round over the bar next to the edge in cream. Leave four bars uncovered and work a bar across the mesh, leave one bar uncovered and work a second line across. Cut out the large uncovered area taking care to leave one bar beside the tent stitch. Overcast the inner edge in main colour wool. Fill in the remaining mesh with tent stitch in main colour.

8 To prepare the card for the sides see page 114/L. Slip stitch to the prepared mesh using matching sewing thread. Repeat for the base, this time omitting the wadding.

MAKING UP AND LINING THE BOX
Use edge stitch in doubled-up Pearl cotton and follow the instructions on page 116/O and pages 116–117/P. When lining the box, cover the 2mm card for the sides with patterned fabric and the base with plain fabric.

MAKING THE LID
Follow the instructions on page 115/M.

FITTING THE BOX
The box shown in the photograph has a built-in pin box and pincushion. For this you will need a shallow plastic box. (I used the lid of a slide box which measures 2½ x 3¾ x ⅞in (64 x 95 x 22mm) deep.) Find a suitable box and if necessary adjust the measurements to suit it.

1 To make the tray, see pages 117–118/Q.

2 To make the fabric-covered needlecase, see page 119/S.

Blue Print Square Box
❑ ❑

This elegant box has a more unusual shape than most. The Laura Ashley furnishing fabric used to cover it is a wonderful bold print which is fairly heavy and firm. Unlike the method used in the large fabric sewing box, the fabric for the sides of this box is cut in one piece, with a join at the centre back. The lid is a fit-on type with a lip.

MATERIALS
Plastic canvas: ultra-stiff, 7-count, two sheets
   12 x 18in (305 x 457mm)
2mm card, 7 x 22in (178 x 560mm)
Thin card, 7 x 18in (178 x 457mm)
Fabrics: ½yd/m patterned and ¼yd/m lining
2oz wadding, ¼yd/m
Anchor Pearl cotton, 5gm skeins – five dark and
   two light, to tone with fabric
Sewing thread to tone with main colour

PREPARATION
1 Cutting the plastic canvas
Base, underlid and lid: Cut three (44 bars) square. Cut a triangle with sides of 11 bars off one corner of each as shown (in fig 1), leaving two sides 33 bars long.

Sides: Cut two (18 x 44 bars), two (18 x 33 bars) and one (18 x 16 bars).
Lid lip: Cut two (3 x 40 bars), two (3 x 29 bars) and one (3 x 15 bars).
Tray base: Cut one 40 bars square.
Tray sides: Cut two (6 x 40 bars), two (6 x 18 bars) and two (6 by 23 bars).

2 Cutting the card
2mm card:
Base lining: Cut one 6⁵⁄₁₆in (160mm) square.
Box lining the sides: Cut one 2½ x 6⅜in (64 x 162mm), one 2½ x 6¼in (64 x 158mm), two 2½ x 4½in (64 x 114mm) and one 2⅛ x 2½in (54 x 64mm).
Tray supports: Cut one 1¼ x 6¼in (32 x 158mm), one 1¼ x 6⅛in (32 x 156mm) and two 1¼ x 2⅝in (32 x 67mm).

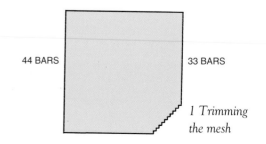

44 BARS   33 BARS

1 Trimming the mesh

Thin card:

Outer base: Cut one 6⁵⁄₁₆in (160mm) square.

Tray: Cut one piece 5¾in (146mm) square.

Lid: Cut one piece 6¼in (158mm) square.

Using the mesh as a guide trim one corner off each of the 2mm and 1mm squares of card for the base, and the inside lid. The edge should be between the two outer bars of the mesh, allowing room for the needle to pass through when stitching up.

3 Cutting the fabric and wadding

Patterned fabric: For the side cut one piece 3¾ x 27in (95 x 686mm). Using the card as a guide and allowing ¾in (19mm) extra all round for turnings, cut fabric to cover the base, the lid, the tray and the four tray supports.

Lining fabric: Using the 2mm cut card as a guide and allowing ¾in (19mm) extra all round for turnings, cut five sides, one piece for the base, one for the inside lid and one for outer base of the tray.

Wadding: For the sides cut one piece 2½ x 26in (64 x 660mm). For the base cut one piece the size of the 2mm card base. For the lid cut three pieces, one the same size as the thin card cut for the lid, one slightly smaller, and one smaller still.

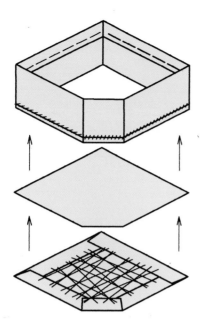

2 Covering the box with fabric and stitching on the base

4   Covering the card

Cover the thin card for the outer base with patterned fabric and the lid lining and box base with lining fabric (see page 114/L).

MAKING UP THE BOX

1   To make the box side, overcast the five side pieces together using a single strand of Pearl cotton.

2   Cover the box side with fabric-covered Vilene and wadding, as described on page 106/E, under 'Fabric Covered Boxes'. The method is the same as that for a circular box with the exception that a layer of wadding is placed between the fabric and the Vilene to give a padded effect.

3   Slip stitch the prepared outer base card to the base mesh. Place right side down with the box side over it, edge stitch to join using the main colour (fig 2).

LINING THE BOX

1   To line the box, see pages 116–117/P.

2   Cover the four tray supports with patterned fabric. Spread adhesive on the back of the longest section and position inside the box. Do the same with the slightly shorter section and position inside the box. Lastly, glue and position the two short supports (fig 3).

MAKING THE LID

1   Work a line of cross stitch in contrast colour all round over the bar next to the edge of the two lid sections. Using the mesh as a guide trim the corner off the 1mm card for the inside lid and cover with the piece of lining fabric.

2   Continue by following the instructions on page 115/M.

MAKING THE FITTINGS

1   Cut a square of 22 bars from one corner of the mesh for the tray (40 x 40 bars). Trim the 1mm and thin card for the tray (5¾in/146mm) square, so that the edges fit just inside the outer bar of the mesh. Cover the thin card with lining fabric and slip stitch to one side of the tray base mesh. Cover the 1mm card with patterned fabric.

2   Embroider the tray sides in a stitch of your choice. (I used long cross stitch for speed. Tent stitch would cover both sides of the mesh better but takes longer to work).

3   Join the corners and edge stitch round the top edge. Place the mesh for the base covered side down with the sides over it and overcast all round to join. Slip the lining in place. Finally, put the tray inside to complete your box.

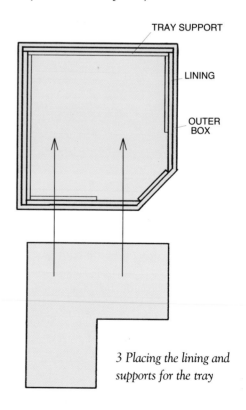

TRAY SUPPORT

LINING

OUTER
BOX

3 Placing the lining and supports for the tray

Medium Rhodes Stitch Box

This box features Rhodes stitch in its design – a stitch that is not only very easy to work but is also exceptionally rewarding as it looks so sumptuous with its bulky finish. There is a choice of double cross stitch or rice stitch to surround and augment the Rhodes stitches. The double cross stitch is quicker to work and also requires less Pearl cotton; the rice stitch, on the other hand, looks a little richer, adding a slightly more luxurious touch.

This box is just the right size to hold two packs of playing cards, pencils and bridge score cards. It is embroidered on 7-count plastic canvas, padded with wadding and lined with fabric-covered card. A smaller version could be made by substituting 10-count plastic canvas and using finer yarns. The side lining is slightly lower than the embroidered mesh, making a recess into which the lid lining fits, while the lid itself is hinged and has a tassel for easy opening. If desired, the box may be personalised by embroidering a name and date on the base.

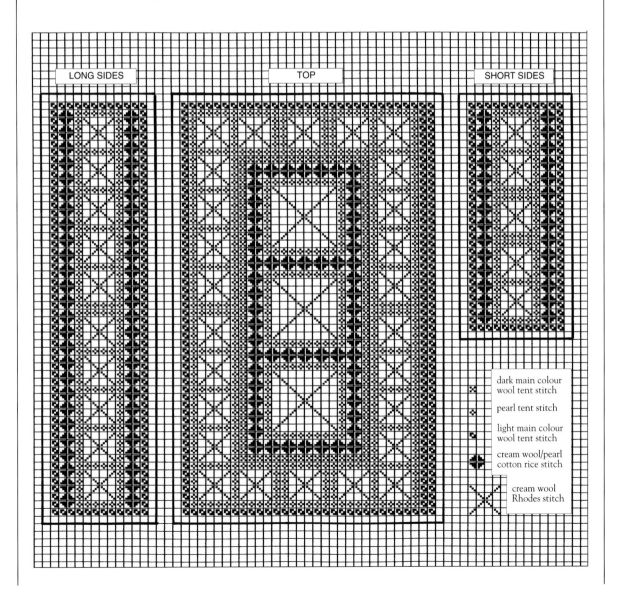

LONG SIDES

TOP

SHORT SIDES

dark main colour wool tent stitch

pearl tent stitch

light main colour wool tent stitch

cream wool/pearl cotton rice stitch

cream wool Rhodes stitch

BASE

Follow the key for the top or use left-over threads to work the base

MATERIALS

Plastic canvas: ultra-stiff 7-count, one sheet 12 x 18in (305 x 457mm)

2mm card, 9 x 17in (230 x 432mm)

Thin card, 4⅝ x 8⅛in (118 x 206mm)

Cotton lining fabric, ¼yd/m

2oz wadding, ¼yd/m

Paterna stranded wool, 8m skeins – three of dark main colour: pink 922, blue 512 or green 602; three of light main colour: pink 923, blue 513 or green 603, and five cream 263

Anchor Pearl cotton No 5, 5gm skeins – three of main colour pink 968, blue 975 or green 213

Squared paper

PREPARATION

1   Cutting the plastic canvas

Box lid: Cut one (33 x 56 bars).

Box base: Cut one (32 x 56 bars).

Box side: Cut two (14 x 56 bars) and two (14 x 32 bars).

2   Cutting the 2mm card

Side lining: Cut two 1⅞ x 8⅛in (47 x 206mm) and two 1⅞ x 4½in (47 x 114mm).

Box base: Cut one 4½ x 8in (114 x 203).

Lid: Cut one 4⅛ x 7⅞in (105 x 196mm).

3   Cutting the fabric

Using the cut pieces of card as a guide, and allowing ¾in (19mm) all round for turning, cut fabric to cover each piece of card.

4   Cutting the wadding

Cut one piece a little smaller than each side mesh, and one a little smaller than the lid mesh.

WORKING THE EMBROIDERY

Work with two strands of wool. Use the Pearl cotton doubled for the tent stitch and single for the rice and double cross stitch. Doubled cotton would look richer but use more thread. Follow charts, working from edge towards centre. Note that the lid is one bar wider than the base. Work two of the long sides and two of the short.

MAKING UP AND LINING THE BOX

Make up the box using edge stitch in dark wool and line it by referring to page 114/L, pages 116/O and 116–117/P, including the wadding between the card lining and the plastic canvas of the sides and lid. See page 121/T for making a tassel.

FITTING THE BOX

To complete your box, fit it following the instructions on pages 117–118/Q.

Large Rhodes Stitch Box

Like the previous project this box also features Rhodes stitch but is larger, measuring 7¼ x 9½ x 2in (184 x 241 x 51mm) deep. It was designed to hold sewing accessories and the fitted tray includes a small needlecase and rests upon two containers suitable for storing pencils or other narrow items. This box would be equally useful for storing lace bobbins, costume jewellery or other personal possessions and the fittings may be readily adapted.

The box is embroidered on 7-count plastic canvas in a mixture of wool and Pearl cotton using a variety of stitches. Wadding is inserted between the plastic canvas and the card linings to heighten the richness of the finished appearance. The lid is hinged and has a tassel, the lid lining fitting into the box to ensure stability.

MATERIALS

Plastic canvas: ultra-stiff 7-count, two sheets 12 x 18in (305 x 457mm)

2mm card, 13 x 19in (330 x 483mm)

Thin card, 10 x 20in (254 x 508mm)

Cotton lining fabric, ½yd/m

2oz wadding, 20in (508mm) square

Flannel or Aida, 2½ x 5in (64 x 127mm) for the needlecase 'page'

Paterna stranded wool, 8m skeins – nine of main colour pink 922, blue 512 or green 602; four of lighter main colour pink 923, blue 513 or green 603 and seven cream 263

Anchor Pearl cotton No 5, 5gm skeins – four of main colour pink 968, blue 975 or green 213

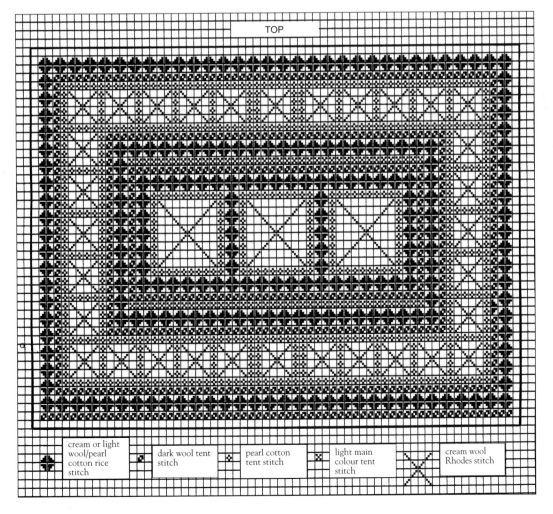

	cream or light wool/pearl cotton rice stitch		dark wool tent stitch		pearl cotton tent stitch		light main colour tent stitch		cream wool Rhodes stitch

PREPARATION

1 Cutting the plastic canvas

Lid: Cut one (45 x 66 bars).

Base: Cut one (44 x 66 bars).

Sides: Cut two (18 x 66 bars) and two (18 x 44 bars).

Tray base: Cut one (39 x 61 bars).

Tray sides: Cut two (6 x 61 bars) and two (6 x 39 bars).

Tray dividers: Cut two (6 x 39 bars) and two (6 x 22 bars).

Tray supports: Cut two (8 x 39 bars), four (6 x 39 bars) and four (6 x 8 bars).

Needlecase covers: Cut two (19 x 19 bars) and one spine (3 x 19 bars).

2 Cutting the card

2mm card:

For the box sides, cut two 2½ x 9¾in (64 x 248mm) and two 2½ x 6¼in (64 x 158mm). For the base and lid, cut one 6¼ x 9½in (158 x 241mm) and one 6⅛ x 9⅜in (159 x 240mm).

Thin card:

For the lid lining, cut one 6½ x 9¾in (165 x 248mm). For the tray interior lining, cut one 3 x 5¾in (76 x 146mm), one 2¼ x 5¾in (57 x 146mm), one 3¼in square (82mm) and one 2¼ x 3¼in (57 x 82mm).

WORKING THE EMBROIDERY

Work with two strands of wool and use the Pearl cotton doubled for the tent stitch and single for the rice and double cross stitch. The doubled cotton looks richer but requires more thread. Follow the charts and for ease in counting, work from the outer edge towards the centre. Work two long sides and two short. The short sides are worked in a similar way to the long, but with just seven Rhodes stitches. Note that the lid is one bar wider than the base. The box may be personalised by stitching a name or initials on the base. Charted alphabets can be found on pages 36 and 78.

MAKING UP, LINING AND FITTING THE BOX

Follow the instructions for the medium Rhodes stitch box, see page 48.

A selection of large and medium Rhodes stitch boxes

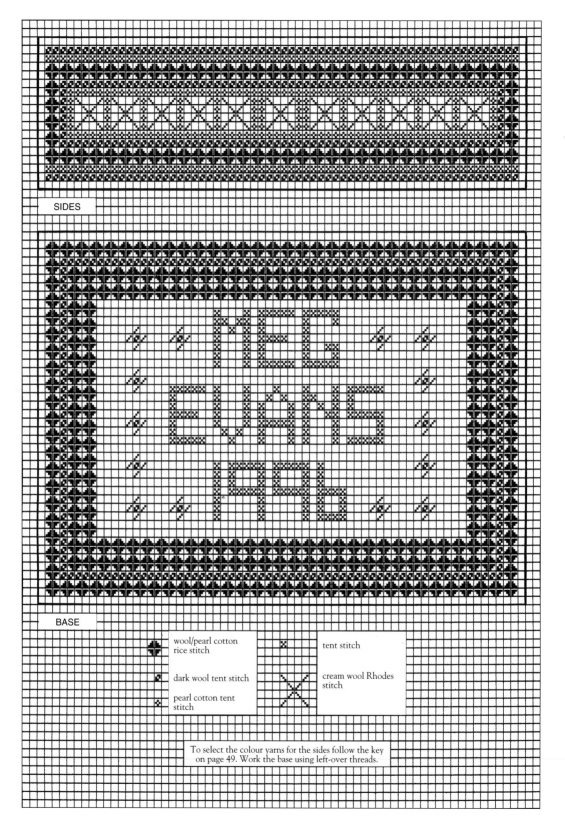

SIDES

BASE

	wool/pearl cotton rice stitch		tent stitch
	dark wool tent stitch		cream wool Rhodes stitch
	pearl cotton tent stitch		

To select the colour yarns for the sides follow the key
on page 49. Work the base using left-over threads.

*Personalise the base of your Rhodes stitch box by stitching a name or initials and a date
following the alphabets charted on pages 36 and 78*

The embroidered base of the large Rhodes stitch box

Embroidered Rectangular Canvas Box

□ □ □ □ □

When making boxes things do not always turn out quite as anticipated, and this box demonstrates this fact admirably. I intended to make it entirely from cotton canvas and card, having a fit-on lid with the edge worked in edge stitch. On completion of the embroidery the lid canvas was slightly distorted, so was stretched (blocked) in the usual way. I completed the box but even when mounted over card the canvas was still a little distorted at the corners. This would not have been noticeable had the lid been of the slip-in variety, but I was not satisfied, so I unpicked the edge stitch and pressed the embroidery and then enclosed it in a frame made of 10-count plastic canvas. To allow for the thickness of the embroidery this lid has sides. As the side was worked in a diagonal stitch this too was slightly distorted and needed stretching. This problem could be avoided by using a long cross instead of the diagonal stitch.

MATERIALS

Cotton canvas: 12 threads per 1in (25mm), one piece 5 x 33in (127 x 838mm) and one 9 x 12in (230 x 305mm)

Plastic canvas: 10-count, one sheet 10½ x 13½in (267 x 343mm)

Cotton lining fabric, ½yd/m

Paterna stranded wool, as listed on the chart key, you will need five skeins of cream, thirteen of spruce, and one of each of the other colours

2oz wadding, ¼yd/m

Craft Vilene, ¼yd/m

2mm card, 20in (508mm) square

1mm card, one piece 5¼ x 8¼in (133 x 210mm), and one 6⅛ x 9 in (155 x 230mm)

Sewing thread to tone with main colour wool

Lacing thread, No 5 crochet cotton, or similar strong thread

12in (305mm) rotating embroidery frame

PREPARATION

1   The cotton canvas

Starting 1½in (38mm) in from the left short edge of the long canvas for the side, mark the area to be embroidered for the sides, using a fabric marker. These sections should be 2⅜in (60mm) deep by 9in (230mm), 6in (152mm), 9in (230mm)

and 6in (152mm), and should have two threads between each of the sections. Frame up the canvas. Mark the centre of the 9 x 12in (230 x 305mm) rectangle of canvas for the lid in both directions. If you have a second frame prepare this too. The side is repetitive work and it is pleasant to have a change from one to the other.

2   Cutting the plastic canvas

Lid: Cut two (63 x 92 bars).

Lid sides: Cut two (3 x 63 bars) and two (3 x 92 bars).

Lid lips: Cut two (4 x 55 bars) and two (4 x 84 bars).

3   Cutting the card

Cut the card as work progresses. Measurements given here are those that I used for the box shown above. Variations are likely in different boxes, check and make adjustments before cutting the card.

WORKING THE EMBROIDERY

Following the chart on page 56, use two strands of wool throughout, unless using small cross stitch for the top, when a single strand should be used.

1   For the side, work two long and two short sides. Work in the main colour in large diagonal stitch, or if preferred in long cross stitch to avoid distortion. Leave the two threads between the sections uncovered. Edge stitch will be worked over these later to form the corners.

2   For the lid, work the embroidery for the top following the chart. Half cross stitch was used in the sample but cross stitch may be used to avoid distortion of the canvas. On completion of the pattern fill in with cream in the appropriate stitch to give an area 6 x 9in (152 x 230mm). If necessary stretch the canvas as described on page 116/N.

3 For the lid frame. For the upper lid, on one section of mesh (63 x 92 bars) starting over the bar next to the edge work two rectangles of tent stitch. Very carefully cut out the central uncovered area, taking care to leave one bar beside the embroidery. Trim off the spikes. Overcast all round the aperture in the main colour. Work tent stitch along the four lid sides.

4 For the underlid, on the other section of mesh (65 x 94 bars), work three rectangles of tent stitch as in step 3. Do not cut out the central area.

5 Work two rows of tent stitch along each of the four lid lips.

MAKING UP AND LINING THE BOX

1 Press the box side embroidery well from the wrong side, stretching (blocking) if necessary. Fold along one set of uncovered threads between the sides, matching up the holes, and work edge stitch (cotton canvas version) along the fold. Repeat twice to make three corners.

2 Lie the embroidery right side down and measure the card needed for each side. In the example these were two 2¼x 9in (57 x 230mm) and two 2¼ x 6in (57 x 152mm). As canvases may vary slightly measure your own carefully. Cut 2mm card to these sizes and chamfer the short edges (see page 117/P).

3 Cut a piece of Vilene the same width as the short edges and 30in (762mm) long. Lie this flat and spread adhesive on the unchamfered side of each piece of card in turn. Place on the Vilene in a line, short edges touching and allow to bond (fig 4a).

4 Tack the short edges of the side embroidery pieces to form the box shape. Place the prepared Vilene-covered card inside and check that the length is correct. Make any necessary alterations then remove the card and tacking.

5 Fold under the short edges of the canvas to the wrong side, leaving one uncovered thread along the fold line. Place the two folded edges together, right sides out, and edge stitch through both layers to join. Fold the uncovered canvas to the wrong side round one edge, so that two threads lie together along the fold, and work edge stitch all round. Repeat with the other edge.

6 Place the card between the embroidery and the canvas turnings, making sure the corners are in their correct places. Starting at the middle of one long side, begin lacing across to hold the turnings. The edge stitch should lie on the narrow edges of the card. If necessary remove the lacing, take the card out and trim to the correct size. Place back in position and lace across completely round the box. Fasten off at one end. Starting at this end, tighten the lacing round the box and fasten off (fig 4b).

7 Cut a piece of card for the base 8⅞ x 6in (225 x 152mm) and cover with lining fabric (see page 114/L). Place the prepared side over it and ladder stitch to join using the toning sewing thread.

8 For lining see page 114/L and page 116/P.

MAKING THE LID

1 With a steam iron press the embroidery from the wrong side over a towel. If necessary stretch (block) to remove any distortion (see page 115/N).

2 Trim the turnings to 1in (25mm) and the corners diagonally to within three threads of the stitching. To make up the lid, see page 115/M, steps 3 to 5.

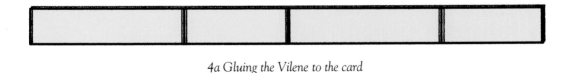

4a Gluing the Vilene to the card

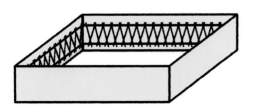

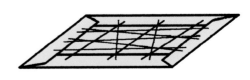

4b Preparing the box side and base

◿	263 cream background
◢	533 spruce
◺	D546 light green
◨	561 dark blue

I	563 light blue
‖	904 dark pink
·	915 light pink
■	321 grape

+	313 mauve
⊠	713 yellow
⊡	444 honey

Embroidered Linen Box

❑ ❑ ❑ ❑

This little box in linen with a pulled work panel is designed to hold a present for a bride. The design exploits the loose weave of the linen for an embroidered insert, which forms an interesting contrast with the plain fabric.

The fabric used is actually sold as dishcloths. Linen ones seem much too good to be used in the kitchen and just cry out to be embroidered. The same fabric is available by the yard from specialist suppliers and is called linen scrim.

The slip-in lid is constructed on a greyboard frame mount. A coloured card mount, as sold in art shops, could be used instead but these are not so thick so would need to be handled with extra care. It is best that you make the lid first and cut the card for the box to fit the lid.

Other types of fabric, not necessarily of loose weave, could be used for the box and combined with a loose weave fabric for the oval panel. Very little of the background fabric for the insert will show, as it is covered with stitching, but the colour should blend well with that of the box fabric.

MATERIALS

2mm greyboard, 10 x 12in (254 x 305mm)
1mm card, 4⅛ x 5¾in (105 x 146mm)
Linen or similar fabric, 21in (533mm) square
Lightweight silk or cotton lining fabric to tone with the linen, ¼yd/m
Lightweight plain cream cotton fabric, ¼yd/m
Anchor stranded cotton, 8m skeins – one cream 387
Anchor Pearl cotton, 8m skeins – two cream 926
Anchor Marlitt (shiny rayon thread), 10m skeins – one cream 1034
Mohair or other textured knitting yarn, 6yd/m
Small amounts of any other cream yarns you have to hand
2oz wadding, ¼yd/m
1½ mm Offray embroidery ribbon, 2yd/m – ivory 810
Frame with an oval aperture, 5⅛ x 6⅝in (130 x 168mm)
Sewing thread to match the linen
Hoop embroidery frame, 6in (152mm)

PREPARATION

1 Cutting the card

Card mount:

For the lid frame, trim a bare ½in (13mm) from four sides of the mount, giving a piece 4⅛ x 5¾in (105 x 146mm).

1mm card:

For the lid lining cut one 4⅛ x 5¾in (105 x 146mm). The remaining pieces should be cut after the lid is complete.

2 Cutting the fabric and wadding

Linen: For the lid, cut two pieces 7 x 9in (178 x 230mm), for the base, cut one piece 6 x 8in (152 x 203mm) and for the side, cut one length 2½ x 23in (64 x 584mm).

Backing fabric: For the lid, cut two pieces 7 x 9in (178 x 230mm), for the base cut one piece 6 x 8in (152 x 203mm) and for the side cut one length 2½ x 24in (64 x 610mm).

Lining: For inside lid and base cut two pieces 5½ x 7in (140 x 178mm), for sides cut two pieces 2 x 7in (50 x 178mm) and two pieces 2 x 6in (50 x 152mm).

Wadding: Cut three pieces the size of the mount aperture.

WORKING THE EMBROIDERY

1 Overcast the edges of the linen fabric for the lid and side to prevent fraying. Run a line of tacking stitches across the two lid pieces in both directions to mark the centre lines.

2 With a pencil mark centre lines on the frame in both directions. Place the frame centrally over one piece of fabric and mark the oval outline to be embroidered with a water-erasable marker or a hard pencil (fig 5a).

3 Cut a 8yd/m length of cream Pearl cotton and put it aside for making a cord later.

4 See the small embroidered box project (page 30) and the stitch directory (pages 122 to 126) for details of the embroidery. The way the yarns are used will vary according to the type. Use the full six strands of stranded cotton. The Pearl cotton and Marlitt thread may be used doubled while the mohair and ribbon should be used singly.

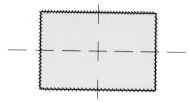

5a Overcasting the edges

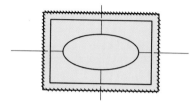

5b Marking the area to be embroidered

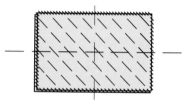

6 Mounting the fabric

5   To embroider the top, mount the fabric onto the hoop frame, or work in the hand if preferred. The area covered should be a little larger, about ¼in (6mm) than the marked shape.

6   Work flower shapes in radiating straight stitches mixing the yarns to give a good variation in texture. Work French knots in between. Very little of the fabric should be visible when the embroidery is complete.

7   If you also wish to embroider the side, work sufficient for two long sides and two short. The length of stitching should be 22in (560mm). Mark the depth of the box on the fabric with lines of tacking and work the embroidery of your choice. In the sample, lines of stem stitch were used in the following sequence:

a) Work a line at the base in stranded cotton.

b) Miss one thread and work a line in Pearl cotton.

c) Miss four threads and work a line in Pearl cotton.

d) Miss three threads and work a line in stranded cotton.

e) Miss two threads and work two adjacent lines in Pearl cotton.

f) Miss two threads and work a line in Pearl cotton.

BACKING THE FABRIC

Lie the side fabric right side down with the relevant backing fabric exactly over it. Smooth it out carefully and then tack at 1in (25mm) intervals to hold together. Repeat the process with the unembroidered fabric for the top. Each double layer will then be treated as one piece (fig 6).

MAKING THE LID

1   Make the lid following the instructions given on page 108/H, and using the lid top described below.

2   Prepare the frame for the lid top as shown below in figs 7a and b. As the pulled work embroidery is naturally domed it will not need to be stretched over card. Spread glue round the aperture on the wrong side of the frame and lie it right side down. Place the embroidery over the aperture, right side down. Check from the right side before allowing to bond. Place the layers of wadding to support the dome, gluing very lightly in place. Fold the turnings over the card and lace in both directions.

3   Cover the lid lining card with lining fabric and then ladder stitch or glue in place over the underside of the lid.

4   Make a twisted cord from the reserved length of Pearl cotton (see page 121/T) and slip stitch it to the lid. Start at the centre of one long

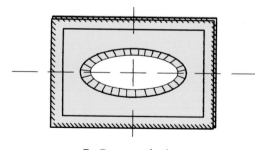

7a Covering the frame

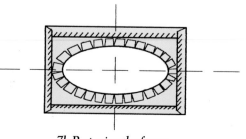

7b Preparing the frame

side, leaving a length of 2in (50mm). When the stitching returns to the centre use doubled Pearl cotton to bind the two ends together, knotting the binding thread at the back and letting the ends hang down to join the others. Separate the strands with a needle and trim off to a suitable length.

MAKING UP AND LINING THE BOX

The following measurements were for my box, so check these against your own lid and make any necessary adjustments to them before cutting, as these may vary according to the fabric being used.

1   For the outer box, cut the 2mm card to give two sides 1 x 6in (25 x 152mm), two sides 1 x 4¼in (25 x 108mm) and one base 4¼ x 5¾in (108 x 146mm). For the lining, cut two sides ¾ x 5¾in (19 x 146mm), two sides ¾ x 3⅞in (19 x 98mm) and one base 3⅞ x 5½in (98 x 140mm).

2   To make up and line the box see pages 116–117/P and pages 109–110/I.

Small Square Fabric Box

This attractive little box is just 4in (102mm) square, and is ideal for filling with a small gift for a friend or family member. The richly-patterned fabric covers a simple card construction, and the whole box can be completed in just a few hours. The following instructions show how to make a hinged lid, however, the project could be made simpler still for a beginner by omitting the hinge and tab – the lid would then simply lift off. Choose a lining fabric to complement the patterned exterior of the box, you can also add a couple of lengths of narrow ribbon and a bow to the lid as a decorative detail.

MATERIALS

2mm card, 8 x 18in (203 x 457mm)

Fabrics: ¼yd/m patterned fabric and ¼yd/m lining fabric to contrast

2oz wadding, ¼yd/m

Craft Vilene, ¼yd/m

9mm ribbon, 1yd/m

Sewing thread to tone with fabric

PREPARATION

1   Cutting the card

Base: Cut one 3⅞in (98mm) square.

Sides: Cut four 2 x 4in (50 x 102mm).

Lid: Cut one 4⅜in (112mm) square.

Base lining: Cut one 3⅝ (92mm) square.

Side lining: Cut two 1⅝ x 3⅞in (41 x 98mm) and two 1⅝ x 3⅝in (41 x 92mm).

For the lid lining: Cut one 3⅝in (92mm) square.

2   Cutting the fabric

When using the card as a guide allow 1in (25mm) extra all round on lid sections, ¾in (19mm) for all other pieces.

Patterned fabric: For the side cut one piece 3¼ x 17¼in (80 x 440mm). Using the card as a guide cut one base and one lid. For the hinge, cut one 4¼ x 7¼in (108 x 184mm), and for the tab, one 1½ x 3in (38 x 76mm).

Contrast: Using the card as a guide cut one lid, one base and four side linings.

3   Cutting the wadding and Vilene

Cut four pieces of wadding the same size as the lid card. Cut one piece of Vilene the same size as the base and one strip 2 x 16in (51 x 432mm).

MAKING UP AND LINING THE BOX

1   Lie the length of Vilene down. Chamfer the short edges of the card (see page 117, fig 17c). Spread adhesive over one side of each piece and place in line on the Vilene. Allow to bond.

2   Continue as on page 66 steps 3, 4 and 5.

3   For lining the box see page 116/P.

MAKING THE LID

1   Place the fabric for the lid right side down, with the four layers of wadding centrally over it followed by the card. Lace in both directions, taking care at the corners to fold the surplus fabric neatly in at a right angle as these will still be visible when the lining is positioned.

2   Cut two pieces of ribbon 7in (178mm) long and place across the lid, stitching or gluing the ends to the underside card. Make a bow and glue or stitch over the intersection (fig 8).

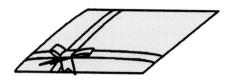

8 Adding the ribbons and bow to the lid

3   Place the tab centrally on the underside of the front edge and glue in place. Glue the free end of the hinge in place centrally on the back edge of the underside of the lid. Glue or stitch the lid lining centrally in place.

4   Insert the box lining then ladder stitch the lid to the box back, working from the back of the box (fig 9).

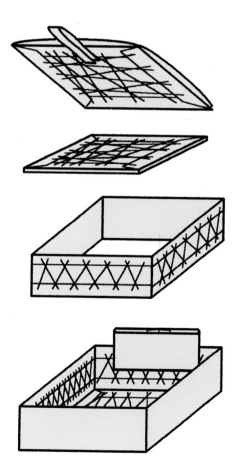

9 Assembling the box and attaching the lid

Christmas Napkin Box

This box would make a special gift for the friend who has everything. Large enough to hold a pack of brightly-coloured paper napkins, it is 7in (178mm) square and will certainly add to the general air of festivity in the dining room at Christmas. It is constructed with card and is covered with pretty seasonal fabric. The lid, which has sides, fits over the box.

MATERIALS
2mm card, 18 x 32in (457 x 813mm)

Fabrics: ½yd/m Christmas print and ½yd/m lining fabric in red or other toning, plain colour

2oz wadding, ½yd/m

Sewing thread to tone with fabrics

Craft Vilene, ½yd/m

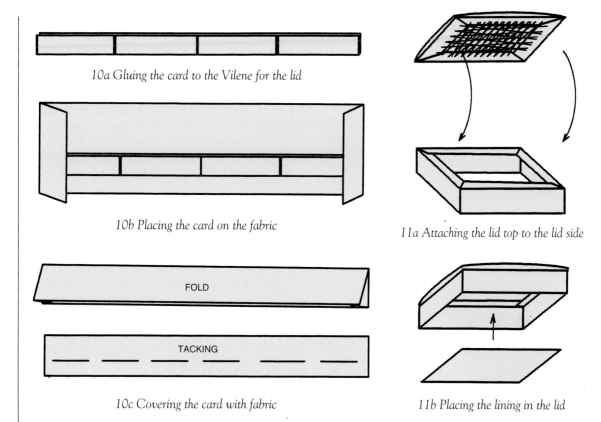

10a Gluing the card to the Vilene for the lid

10b Placing the card on the fabric

FOLD

TACKING

10c Covering the card with fabric

11a Attaching the lid top to the lid side

11b Placing the lining in the lid

PREPARATION

1 Cutting the card

Base: Cut one 6⅞in (174mm) square.

Sides: Cut four 3 x 7in (76 x 178mm).

Base lining,: Cut one 6⅝in (168mm) square.

Side linings: Cut two 2⅞ x 6⅞in (73 x 174) and two 2⅞ x 6⅝in (73 x 168mm).

Lid: Cut one 7⅜in (188mm) square.

Lid sides: Cut four 1 x 7⅜in (25 x 188mm).

Lid lining: Cut one 7⅛in (188mm) square.

2 Cutting the fabric

Patterned fabric:

Side: Cut one 5 x 30in (127 x 762mm).

Base and lid, cut two 10in (254mm) square.

Lid sides: Cut one 3¼ x 31½in (82 x 800mm).

Plain fabric: For the sides, cut four 4 x 8in (102 x 203mm).For the base and lid, cut one of each 9in (230mm) square.

3 Cutting the wadding and the Vilene

Cut four pieces of wadding the same size as the card for the lid, 7⅜in (188mm) square. Cut one piece of Vilene 3 x 28in (76 x 712mm). Cut one piece the same size as the outer base card, the lid sides, the inner base card, the lid lining and the four side card linings.

MAKING UP AND LINING THE BOX

For making up and lining the box, follow the instructions given on page 61.

MAKING THE LID

1   Lie the length of Vilene for the lid side down. Chamfer the short edges of the card (see pages 116–117/P). Spread adhesive over one side of the cards for the lid sides and place in line on the Vilene. Then allow to bond (fig 10a).

2   Fold the fabric for the lid side in half lengthways, right sides outside, and press lightly. Place flat with the wrong side up. Lie the prepared card over this, the edge of the card against the fold line. Fold each short edge over the card and glue lightly in place (fig 10b). Re-fold the fabric over the card and tack close to the card through both layers to hold them in place (fig 10c). Place the short edges together and ladder stitch the seam.

3   Lie the lid fabric right side down with the wadding centrally over it followed by the card. Lace in both directions (see page 115/N). Place over the lid side (fig 11a). Ladder stitch in place. Complete the lid by gluing the lining inside to cover the turnings (fig 11b).

Hexagonal Floral-Print Box
□ □ □ □ □

This lovely box is made with a hinged lid which is slightly bigger than the base, the lid lining fitting inside the box. It is covered with floral striped fabric with the pattern running round the side. The top is made from six triangular sections in a patchwork technique. As the lid (shown on page 39) extends over the sides of the box its exact size is not vital so all the card may be cut before starting work.

MATERIALS
2mm card, 20 x 36in (508 x 915mm)
Fabrics: ½yd/m suitably patterned and ½yd/m contrasting plain-coloured lining fabric
2oz wadding, ¼yd/m
Thin card, 9in (230mm) square
One button (to be covered with fabric)
Craft Vilene, ¼yd/m
Sewing thread in a toning colour

PREPARATION
To mark and cut a hexagon first draw a circle of the desired radius. Then, taking care not to let the compass change size, mark arcs all round the circumference. Draw lines joining the intersection points to form the hexagon. Cut carefully on these lines (fig 12).

1 Cutting the card
2mm card:
Base: Cut a hexagon based on a 4¼in (108mm) radius circle.
Base and lid lining: Cut two hexagons very slightly smaller – a bare ¹⁄₁₆in (1.5mm) less.

Lid: Cut a hexagon based on a 4½in (114mm) circle.
Side: Cut one strip 3¼ x 25½in (82 x 648mm).
Side lining: Cut one strip 3³⁄₁₆ x 25¼in (81mm x 641mm).

2 Cutting the fabric
Patterned fabric: For the side, lay the card in the right position over the striped pattern and cut out allowing ¾in (19mm) extra all round for turnings. For the base lay the card over the fabric, taking the pattern into consideration and cut out allowing ¾in (19mm) extra all round. Reserve the remaining fabric for cutting the lid later.
Plain fabric: Inside lid and base: Cut two pieces using a card hexagon as a guide, allowing ¾in (19mm) extra all round for turnings.
Side lining: Using the card as a guide, cut one piece on the cross, allowing ¾in (19mm) all round for turnings.
Hinge: Cut one piece 3 x 7½in (76 x 190mm).
Stays: Cut two pieces 1 x 6in (25 x 152mm).

3 Cutting the Vilene
Use the side sections and the two larger hexagons as a guide to cut the Vilene to the same size.

MAKING UP THE BOX
Follow the instructions on page 118/R for making a hinge, tab and stays and attaching a button.

1 Spread adhesive sparingly over the hexagon for the base and cover with Vilene. Then cover

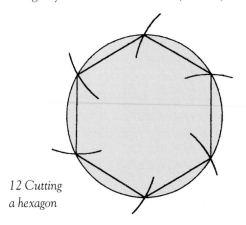

12 Cutting a hexagon

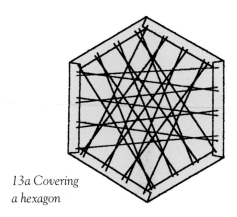

13a Covering a hexagon

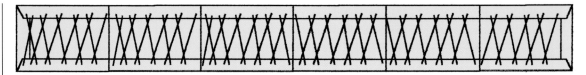

13b Lacing the fabric over the side

with patterned fabric(see page 114/L), lacing the sides on the straight grain first (fig 13a).

2   Mark the card for the side at 4¼in (108mm) intervals, scoring on each line. To do this place a steel rule against the line and cut gently with a craft knife. Cut a second time with slightly more pressure, to cut almost halfway through the card. Spread adhesive sparingly on the scored side and cover with Vilene.

3   Lie the fabric for the side right side down with the card centrally over it, Vilene side down. Starting at the centre lace the turnings. Check that the pattern is correctly placed. Adjust the position if necessary then tighten the lacing (fig 13b). At each end fold the fabric over the card and tuck neatly under the turnings and spot glue. Fasten off.

4   Fold the prepared side with the short edges together, right side outside and ladder stitch to join the seam. Try to keep the hexagonal shape while you do this to get the right tension on the stitches.

5   Lie the base right side down with the side over it and ladder stitch to join (fig 13c).

6   Stitch or glue the hinge to the back (nearest the corner that is ladder stitched), and one end of the stays halfway along the adjacent sides (fig 13d).

LINING THE BOX

1   Prepare the side lining card by following step 2 above, marking at 4⅛in (105mm) intervals.

2   Next glue the Vilene to the unscored side of the card and cover with lining fabric.

3   Place the short ends together with the fabric inside and ladder stitch to join. Place inside the box, with the join opposite the hinge, where it will not be conspicuous, covering the hinge and stays.

4   Ladder stitch all round the top edge of the box, sewing through the hinge and stays.

5   Try the hexagon for the box base lining in position, and, if necessary, adjust the size to improve the fit. Cover with Vilene and lining fabric and slip inside the box.

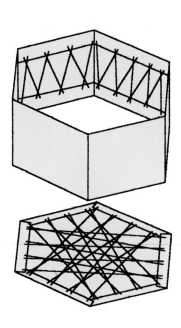

13c Stitching up the box

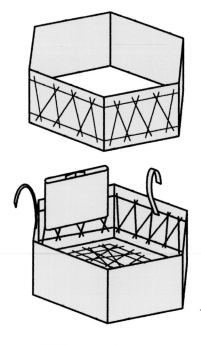

13d Placing the hinge and stays

MAKING THE LID

1 Make two holes at the centre of the lid about ¼in (6mm) apart for stitching on the button.

2 To make the patchwork, start by using the card for the lid as a guide, drawing round it to mark the hexagon on the thin card. Draw lines across from each corner to mark the six triangles. Cut out one of these triangles and use as a template to decide where exactly you wish to place the pattern.

On the back of the fabric place the template in position and mark the outline with a dotted line in pencil. Mark a solid line ⅜in (10mm) from the long edges and 1½in (38mm) from the short (fig 14a). Mark six pieces and cut out on the solid lines. These may be joined by machine or with a small hand backstitch.

Join three patches along the dotted lines to make half the hexagon (fig 14b) and press the seams open. Repeat with the other three patches. Join the final seam and press open (fig 14c).

3 Using the full-size card hexagon as a guide, cut three pieces of wadding the same size. Lie the pieced fabric right side down with the layers of wadding centrally over it and the card on top. Fold the turnings over the card, taking particular care that the joins are at the corners, and lace in position. Cover and stitch the button in place, then stitch or glue the tab to the centre of the front edge.

4 Hold the lid so that the edge opposite the tab is against the hinged edge of the box and spot glue the hinge to the lid. Close the lid to make sure the position is correct, adjusting if necessary so that the lid has an equal overhang all round. When satisfied slip stitch the lid invisibly along the edge of the box and also to the hinge. Spot glue the stays halfway along the two sides adjacent to the hinge. The exposed length will need to be about 3½in (89mm) long. Next test the way the lid opens and make any necessary adjustments.

5 Test the card for the lid lining for size – it should slip comfortably into the box. Adjust if necessary and cover with lining fabric. Spot glue to the centre of the lid. Check that all is well and then ladder stitch to the lid.

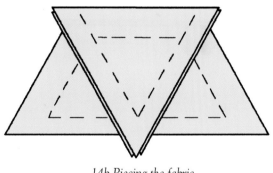

14b Piecing the fabric

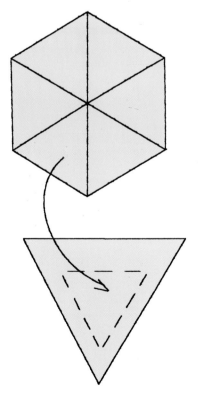

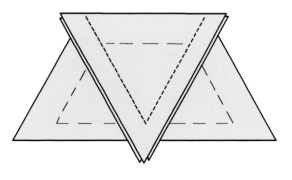

14a Drawing the template　　　　*14c One half of the patchwork*

Drop-Sided Boxes

*T*his type of box is extremely popular and for good reason as the design is so clever and useful. The lids of these boxes fit over the sides holding them in place, but when the lid is removed the sides drop down to reveal the contents. The sides may be separate as they are in the square boxes, or connected by gussets as in the hexagonal box.

The first two boxes in this section are particularly impressive, with great scope for colour customising the embroidery. They are made on 10- and 7-count plastic canvas respectively in mixed wool and Pearl cotton. Both are lined with card but stiff mesh could be used instead to make the box completely washable.

The fabric box with the carnation motif would look wonderful as part of a matching decor in a bedroom or sitting room. It is constructed from card with a lid framed in plastic canvas. The hexagonal box is made entirely of fabric and card and illustrates how the techniques used in the other boxes can be mixed. The elasticated bands and pockets on the sides of the hexagonal box could equally well be used in the square boxes.

Drop-sided boxes are ideal for keeping sewing items neatly, as the pink tulip-motif box (bottom right) shows, the cross stitch sewing box (bottom left) and 'spot' flower-print box (centre) also open in the same way. The hexagonal sewing-print box (top left) is a more elaborate version of the same idea

Tulip Motif Embroidered Box

❏ ❏ ❏

The embroidered tulip motif on this pretty drop-sided box will be eye-catching whichever of the three colourways you choose, be it the green, coffee or pink. It is embroidered directly on 10-count plastic canvas with a thick card lining which gives good stability. The background is worked in stranded wool with the design picked out in Pearl cotton, giving a pleasing contrast in texture. The border is in tied cross stitch with the central design in tent and reverse tent stitch. The lid fits over the side of the box.

MATERIALS

Plastic canvas: 10-count, two sheets 10½ x 13½ in (267 x 343mm)

2mm card, 5 x 17in (127 x 432mm)

1mm card, 5 x 17in (127 x 432mm)

Cotton or polyester/cotton lining fabric, 5½ x 44in (140 x 1118mm)

2oz wadding, ¼yd/m

6mm ribbon, 1yd/m to tone with main colour

Paterna stranded wool, 8m skeins as listed below

Anchor Pearl cotton No 5, 5gm skeins as listed below

Sewing thread in a toning colour

Squared paper

Yarn suggestions

Green version: Paterna stranded wool – five skeins light green 663, three dark green 662, six cream 263; Pearl cotton – two light peach 08, one medium peach 10, one dull peach 338

Pink version: Paterna stranded wool – five skeins light pink 931, one dark pink D211, two green 662, six cream 263; Pearl cotton – two light blue 976, one medium lavender 939, one pink 894

Coffee version: Paterna stranded wool – five skeins dark coffee 472, one light coffee 474, two green 662, six cream 263; Pearl cotton – two light peach 08, one medium peach 10, one dull peach 338

PREPARATION

1 Cutting the plastic canvas

Base: Cut one (42 bars) square.

Box sides: Cut four (45 x 42 bars).

Inner box base: Cut one (18 bars) square.

Inner box sides: Cut four (32 x 18 bars).

Inner box space: Cut one (13 bars) square.

Thimble box: Cut five (12 bars) square.

Thimble box lining: Cut five (10 bars) square.

Lid: Cut one (44 bars) square.

Lid sides: Cut four (9 x 44 bars).

2 Cutting the card

2mm card:

Sides: Cut four 3⅞ x 4⅛in (98 x 105mm).

1mm card:

Base lining: Cut one 3⅞in (98mm) square.

Lid lining: Cut one 4in (102mm) square.

Inner box sides: Cut four 1½ x 2⅞in (39 x 73mm).

3 Cutting the fabric and wadding

When cutting the fabric, use the relevant cut card as a guide and allowing ⅝in (16mm) extra all round for turnings, cut four outer box, four inner box, one base and one lid lining. Using the cut card as a guide cut eight side pieces of wadding the same size.

WORKING THE EMBROIDERY

Follow the charts on page 73 (the yarn variations are given in brackets on the chart key). Use two strands of wool or double thickness of Pearl cotton for the tent stitch and a single strand for the cross stitch lettering on the base. Plan the required lettering (see pages 36 and 78) and work it in cross stitch in the main colour wool or spare Pearl cotton, used singly. Work a border of tied cross and tent stitch, and fill in between this and the central design in cream tent stitch. Work four each of the box sides, inner box sides, thimble box, and lid sides, and five thimble linings.

The pink and green tulip motif embroidered boxes

COVERING THE CARD

1　To cover the card, mark the centre of the card for the eight sides. Draw a line on each side to mark the centre for the ribbon placement. Lie the side lining right side down with the wadding centrally on top, and the card on top of this. Turn the surplus fabric over the edge and lace or glue into position, taking care to set the turnings in slightly at the corners so they will not show.

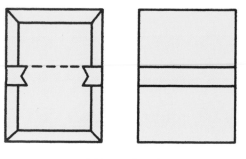

1 Lining the sides

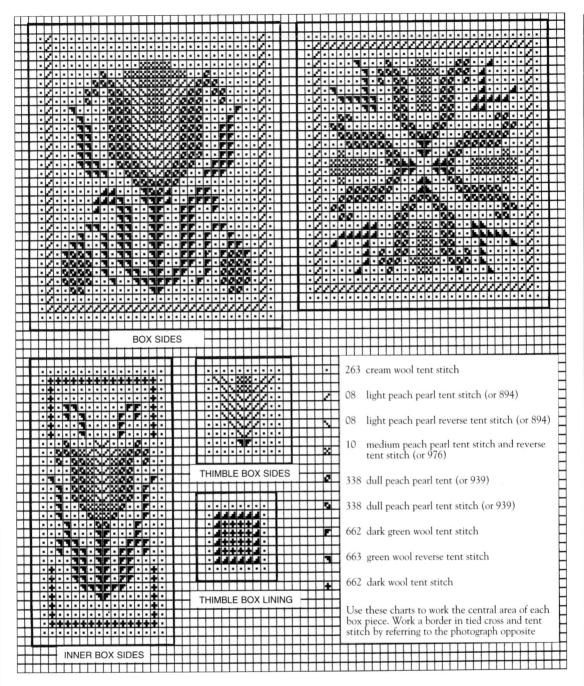

BOX SIDES

THIMBLE BOX SIDES

THIMBLE BOX LINING

INNER BOX SIDES

·	263 cream wool tent stitch
⁄	08 light peach pearl tent stitch (or 894)
⁄	08 light peach pearl reverse tent stitch (or 894)
⊠	10 medium peach pearl tent stitch and reverse tent stitch (or 976)
◩	338 dull peach pearl tent (or 939)
◪	338 dull peach pearl tent stitch (or 939)
⌐	662 dark green wool tent stitch
◥	663 green wool reverse tent stitch
+	662 dark wool tent stitch

Use these charts to work the central area of each box piece. Work a border in tied cross and tent stitch by referring to the photograph opposite

2   Cut the ribbon the width of each side, plus ⅝in (16mm) turnings at each end. Lie a length centrally over the right side of each side section, and stitch or glue the turning to the wrong side.

3   Cover the card for the base and lid linings with fabric only.

STITCHING UP THE BOX

Use a single strand of main colour wool for edge stitching and for joining the box sections and

2a Stitching up the thimble box

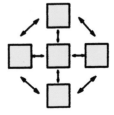

use two strands of wool for overcasting.

1   Using two strands of main colour overcast the four sides of the thimble box to the base (fig 2a), right sides outside. Join the four corners to make a box shape. Repeat with the five pieces for the lining, this time with the right sides inside. Slip this lining into the outer box and overcast together round the top (fig 2b).

2b Inserting the lining in the thimble box

2   Edge stitch round three edges of each outer box side, omitting the base edge. Position one side against the base, wrong sides facing, uncovered edges matched up, and edge stitch to join. Repeat to join the other three sides to the base (fig 2c). Stitch up the inner box in the same way.

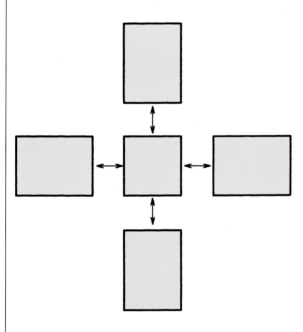

2c Attaching the box sides to the base

3   Glue the lined card in position on the box and inner box sides. The edges should be level at the top, and slightly set in at the sides so that when the box is closed the edges of the embroidered mesh will fit neatly together and the lining will be completely hidden.

4   Glue the covered base lining card centrally onto the base, then glue the thimble box to the base of the inner box. Finally, glue the inner box in position at 45 degrees to the base of the outer box (fig 2d).

2d Assembling the box

MAKING THE LID

1   Lie one lid side against the lid, right sides outside, and with the uncovered edges matched up, and edge stitch to join. Repeat with the other three sides (fig 3).

2   Overcast the corners to join. Edge stitch all round the free edge, matching the colours. To finish, place the lined card inside the lid and glue or slip stitch in place.

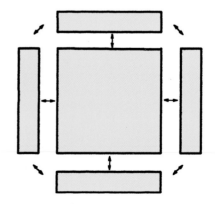

3 Stitching up the lid

Cross Stitch Sewing Box

This elegant drop-sided box is relatively quick and easy to make. It is based on 7-count plastic canvas and like the previous box has a thick card lining which gives good stability. The use of two-colour cross stitch in a mixture of wool and Pearl cotton adds interest to the work and a delightful contrast in texture. The techniques used are the same as for the previous project with the exception of the thimble holder, which is unlined and stitched directly to the inner box base.

MATERIALS

Plastic canvas: standard or ultra-stiff 7-count, one sheet 12 x 18in (305 x 457mm)
2mm card, 5 x 17in (127 x 432mm)
1mm card, 5 x 15in (127 x 380mm)
Cotton lining fabric, 5½ x 44in (140 x 1118mm)
2oz wadding, ¼yd/m
Paterna stranded wool, 8m skeins – five dark lavender-blue 560, five light lavender-blue 561, four cream 263
Anchor Pearl cotton No 5, 5gm skeins – three pink 969 and three lavender 939
Strong thread for lacing
9mm Offray embroidery ribbon, 1yd/m antique blue 338

PREPARATION

1 Cutting the canvas

Box base: Cut one (30 x 30 bars).
Box sides: Cut four (30 x 30) bars.
Box lid: Cut one (32 x 32 bars).
Lid sides: Cut four (32 x 6 bars).
Inner box base: Cut one (13 x 13 bars).
Inner box sides: Cut four (22 x 13 bars).
Thimble box sides and base: Cut four (7 x 7 bars).

2 Cutting the card

2mm card:
Side linings: Cut four 4⅛in (105mm) square.
1mm card:
Base lining: Cut one 4⅛in (105mm) square.
Lid lining: Cut one 4½in (114mm) square.
Inner box linings: Cut four 1⅝ x 2⅞in (41 x 73mm).

3 Cutting the fabric and wadding

When cutting the fabric use the relevant piece of cut card as a guide and, allowing ¾in (19mm) extra all round for turnings on the larger pieces, 5⅝in (16mm) on the smaller, cut four box side linings, four inner box side linings, one lid lining and one base lining. Using the cut card as a guide, cut wadding the exact size of the four side lining sections, the four inner box linings and one piece the size of the lid lining card.

WORKING THE EMBROIDERY

Follow the charts on pages 76 and 78, and see the photograph on page 78. Use four strands of wool for the large cross stitch, three for the tent stitch and two for the edge stitch. Use three strands of Pearl cotton for the cross stitch and overcasting and two for the tent stitch. You will need to work four each of the sides, lid sides, inner box sides and thimble box sides, and one lid, base, and inner box base .

MAKING UP THE BOX

Lie one thimble box side over the inner box base, wrong side against right side of base, along the uncovered bar. Overcast to join in dark lavender-blue wool. Do not fasten off but continue to join the other three sides in the same way. Overcast the corners to join into a box shape and overcast round the upper edge (fig 4). Follow the instructions for the tulip motif embroidered box, starting on page 72 for details on assembling the inner and outer boxes. Overcast the edges of the lid top using three strands of pink Pearl cotton.

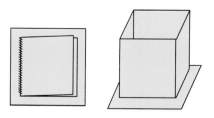

4 Stitching up the thimble box

75

BOX SIDES

LID

BOX BASE

LID SIDES

INNER BOX SIDES

INNER BOX BASE

THIMBLE BOX SIDES

969 pink pearl
tent stitch

263 cream wool
tent stitch

560 dark lavender-blue
cross stitch

Large double cross stitch.
Outer border dark wool and
lavender pearl, inner areas
light wool and pink pearl.

Fill in between the large
cross stitches with straight
cross over two bars in cream

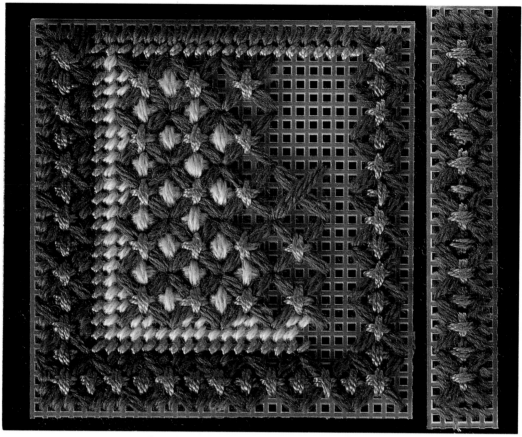

Working the embroidery: side (left) and lid side (right)

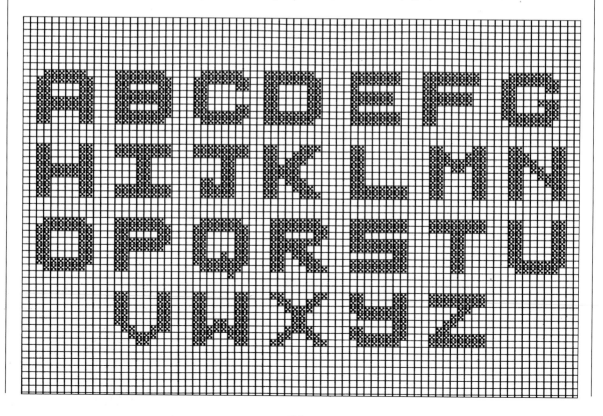

'Spot' Flower-Print Box

The pretty 'spot' carnation design on this fabric is an ideal size for this drop-sided box and is enhanced by the simple patchwork top. The box section is made entirely from fabric and card. The lid fits over the side of the box and is based on plastic canvas, which makes it very easy to construct, the joining stitching of the lid giving a pleasing contrast in texture. If preferred, the lid could be made entirely from fabric and card, as in the Hexagonal Sewing-Print box. The thimble box is made from plastic canvas, but again this could be made from fabric and card. The box could also be made with an all-over print pattern.

MATERIALS

Plastic canvas: 7-count, one sheet 10½ x 13½in (267 x 343mm)

2mm card, 9 x 18in (230 x 457mm)

1mm card, 10 x 12in (254 x 305mm)

Fabrics: ¼yd/m patterned (if using a 'spot' pattern extra fabric may be needed) and ¼yd/m plain cotton lining fabric

2oz wadding, 1¼yd/m

Anchor Pearl cotton No 5, 5gm skeins – two dark and one light, to tone with the fabric

9mm ribbon, 1yd/m

Craft Vilene, 4 x 15in (102 x 380mm)

Sewing thread in a toning colour

PREPARATION

1　Cutting the plastic canvas

Lid: Cut one (28 bars) square.

Lid sides: Cut four (6 x 28 bars).

Thimble holder: Cut five (7 bars) square.

2　Cutting the card

2mm card:

Sides: Cut four 3⅞ x 4¼in (98 x 108mm).

Side linings: Cut four 3⅝ x 4⅛in (92 x 105mm).

1mm card:

Base: Cut two 3⅞in (98mm) square.

Lid lining: Cut one 4in (102mm) square.

Inner box sides: Cut four 1½ x 2⅞in (38 x 73mm).

Inner box side lining: Cut four 1⅜ x 2¾in (35 x 70mm).

Inner box base: Cut one 1½in (38mm) square and one 1¾in (44mm) square.

3　Cutting the fabric and wadding

When using the card as a guide allow ¾in (19mm) extra all round for turnings on the larger pieces, and ⅜in (10mm) on the smaller.

Patterned: If the fabric has a 'spot' motif make templates as described on page 10. Using these as guides cut four pieces for the sides and four for the inner sides. Cut four lid sides 1¼ x 4¼in (32 x 108mm) and one piece the size of the lid mesh.

Plain: Cut four box side linings, four inner box side linings, one base lining and one lid lining. For the patchwork, cut two pieces 1½ x 10in (38 x 254mm).

Wadding: Using the card as a guide, cut two pieces the exact size of the eight card sections.

WORKING THE EMBROIDERY

Use the Pearl cotton doubled.

1　For the lid, work a line of cross stitch in cream all round the lid (28 x 28 bars) over the bar next to the edge. Very carefully cut away the uncovered mesh at the centre taking care to leave one bar inside the embroidery. Trim off the spikes and edge stitch all round the inner edge.

2　For the thimble box, work a line of cross stitch along the top edge over the bar next to the edge of four pieces of mesh (7 x 7 bars). Fill in each one with cross stitch in main colour Pearl cotton. Cover the fifth piece with cross stitch in the main colour. Lie one side section, edge opposite the cream cross stitch against the base, wrong side against right side of base and edges matched up, and overcast to join. Without fastening off continue joining the other three sides in the same way. Overcast the corners to make a box shape, then overcast all round the top edge.

MAKING UP THE BOX

The box is made up in a similar way to the tulip motif embroidered box, page 70.

1　Cover the outer box sides with wadding and fabric, turning the fabric over the card on three

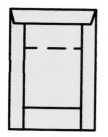
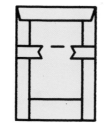

5a Covering the sides   *5b Attaching the ribbon*

sides only, and leaving the lower edge free. If a spot pattern is being used this must be placed carefully in the correct position (fig 5a).

2 Cover the four box side linings with wadding and plain fabric, placing the ribbon as before (fig 5b). Cover the two pieces of the base card with plain fabric, see page 114/L.

3 Lie the covered outer base right side down and place one prepared box side in position with the turning extending over the base. Slip stitch or glue the turnings in place. Repeat for the other three sides (fig 5c).

4 Glue the side linings in place over the side sections, wrong sides facing. The tops will be level, the sides slightly inset. Check that the box will close properly and that the hinges are neat before allowing to bond.

5 Place the base lining in position, covering the raw edges and stitch or glue into place.

MAKING THE INNER BOX

1 Make the inner box up as for the outer, with the lining fabric on the outer sides and the patterned fabric on the inside, placing the spot pattern carefully. Line the base with patterned fabric.

2 Glue the thimble box to the centre of the inner box. Glue to the prepared outer box base at 45 degrees to the outer box (see fig 2d, page 74).

MAKING THE LID

1 Prepare eight patches in the plain fabric as described on page 112/K. Arrange these round the edge of the fabric which is the size of the lid mesh, placing the corners first and checking their position with the frame. Work a running stitch all round to hold in place (fig 6a).

6a The patchwork

2 The lid sides will be covered with fabric but in order to disguise the mesh on the inside, work tent stitch using a single strand of Cream Pearl cotton, to cover each of the four lid sides (6 x 28 bars). Using a single strand avoids bulk, allowing the lid to slip over the sides easily.

3 Cut four rectangles of Vilene ⅝ x 3⅞in (15 x 98mm). Cover each one with patterned fabric, tacking the turnings to the wrong side and pushing them away from the corners so that they will not show. Slip stitch invisibly to each lid side.

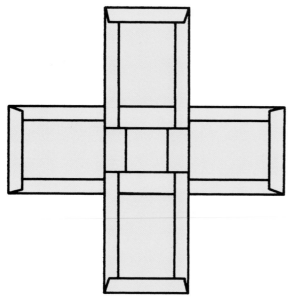

5c Attaching the sides to the base

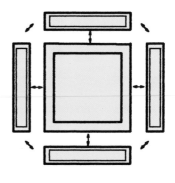

6b Stitching up the lid

4 Lie one lid side against the lid, edges matched up, and edge stitch to join, continuing to join the other three sides in the same way (fig 6b). Work edge stitch to join the corners and then all round the lower edge.

5 Line the square of card for the lid lining with plain fabric. Mount the prepared patchwork on the lid lining as described on page 105/C. Spot glue close to the edge, taking care that this will not show in the aperture, and place behind the lid frame (fig 6c). Slip stitch invisibly. Your box is now complete.

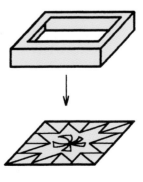

6c The lid

Hexagonal Sewing Print Box

□ □ □ □ □

What nicer way could there be to store your sewing things than in this unusual drop-sided box? Made of card covered in a pretty sewing motif print, it measures 7in (178mm), has hinged sides which are joined by gussets and when the fit-over lid is removed these fall back to give easy access to the contents.

MATERIALS
2mm card, 24in (610mm) square
Fabrics: ½yd/m patterned and ¼yd/m plain
2oz wadding, 9 x 36in (230 x 914mm)
Craft Vilene, ¼yd/m
Sewing thread to tone with patterned fabric
Elastic, 1yd/m, ¼in (6mm) wide

PREPARATION
To mark and cut a hexagon first draw a circle of the desired radius. Then, taking care not to let the compass change size, mark arcs all round the circumference. Draw lines joining their intersection points to form the hexagon. Cut carefully on these lines (see page 64).

1　Cutting the 2mm card
Base: Cut one hexagon using a 3¼in (82mm) radius and inner base very slightly smaller.
Lid and lid lining: Cut one hexagon using a 3½in (89mm) radius and one using a 3⅜in (86mm).
Sides: Cut six 3¾ x 3¼in x (95 x 82mm).
Lining: Cut six 3½ x 3in (89 x 76mm).
Lid sides: Cut six 1 x 3½in (25 x 89mm).

2　Cutting the fabric
Patterned: Using the appropriate cut card as a guide, cut one hexagon for the base and one for the lid, allowing 1in (25mm) extra all round for turnings.

In the same way cut six pieces for the sides, allowing ¾in (19mm) extra all round for turnings. For the lid side cut one 3½ x 21¾in (89 x 552mm). For the pockets cut three 4 x 7in (102 x 178mm). For the bands cut three 2¼ x 6in (57 x 152mm). For the gussets use the template to cut six pieces (see page 85).
Plain: Using the cut card as a guide, cut one hexagon for the base lining, one for the lid lining and six side lining pieces, allowing ¾in (19mm) all round for turnings.

3　Cutting the Vilene and wadding
Using the cut card as a guide, cut six pieces of Vilene the same size as the outer box sides, six the size of the side linings, one the size of the base and inner lid hexagons and one 1 x 21in (25 x 533mm) for the lid side. Cut four pieces of wadding for the lid the exact size of the lid hexagon.

MAKING UP THE BOX
1 Using adhesive sparingly, cover one side of each piece of card with Vilene. On the wrong side of the lining card draw a line just above the centre of the longer edge to mark the band and pocket placement.
2 Cover the outer box sides with patterned fabric, then cover the base hexagon with patterned fabric (see page 114/L), lacing or gluing to hold the turnings. Ladder stitch the sides to the base.
3 Cover the card for lining the sides, base and inside lid with plain fabric.
4 For the bands, fold the fabric in half lengthways and machine stitch a ¼in (6mm) seam. Press the seam open (so that the seam is at the centre of one side) and turn to the right side (fig 7a) Machine stitch along each edge. Alternatively the seam may be stitched by hand from the right side to avoid turning through.

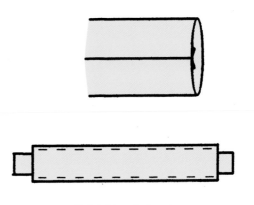

7a Making the bands

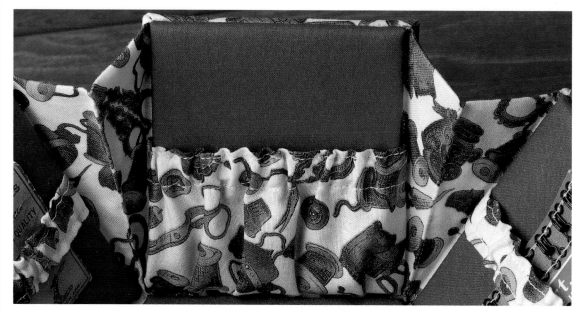

Detail of the interior showing a pocket and two sides with bands

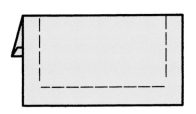

7b The pockets

7c Placing the bands

7d Placing the pockets

5   Cut the elastic into six equal pieces. Using a bodkin, thread one piece into the band. Stretch the required amount – having about 1in (25mm) extending at each end of the band should give the right amount – and stitch to the fabric at each end. Cut off the surplus.

6   For the pockets, fold under and press ¼in (6mm) on one long edge of each of the three pieces of fabric for the pockets. Fold again to make ½in (13mm) turning and machine or hand stitch to secure the turning close to both folded edges (fig 7b). Thread elastic through and secure as for the bands.

7   Place the bands across three side linings 1½in (38mm) down from the top and glue in place to the turnings on the wrong side (fig 7c). Place the pockets in position on the other three sides and glue in place on the wrong side (fig 7d).

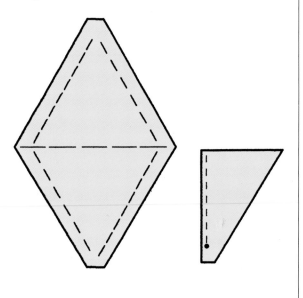

7e The gussets

84

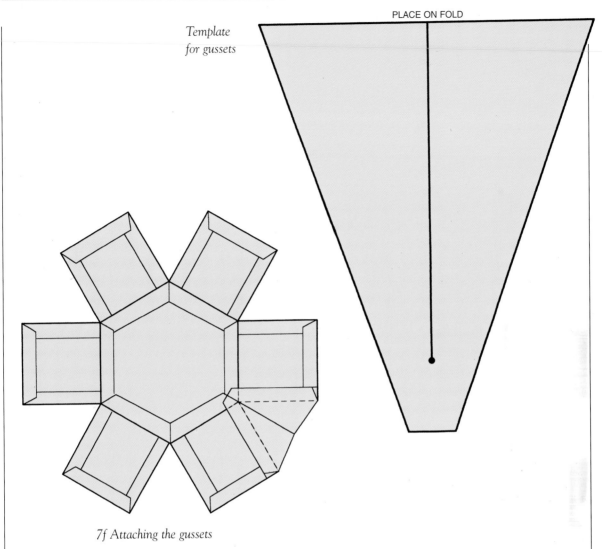

Template for gussets

PLACE ON FOLD

7f Attaching the gussets

8 Fold the gussets in half, right side out, across the shorter centre line, and press. Fold again lengthways, press and machine stitch close to the folded edge to within ¾in (19mm) of the point (fig 7e).

9 Glue the gussets in place between the sides, machine-stitched fold visible on the inside of the box. The points will extend over the base (fig 7f).

10 Place the prepared side linings in position, top edges level, and ladder stitch or glue all round (fig 7g). Glue the lined base centrally over the base.

MAKING THE LID

This lid is made in a similar way to the square fit-over lid on page 63. Follow the instructions given there to make the hexagonal lid for this box, placing the button by referring to page 119/R.

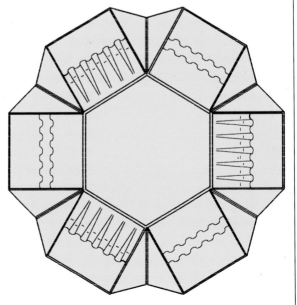

7g The interior of the box

Easy-to-Make Boxes

*O*f it's simplicity, quickness and instant effect you're after then this section is tailor-made for you. None of the boxes in this section is lined, they are all worked from charts and are thus simple to make. In particular the three smaller projects, the bold square box, the embroidered 'matchbox', and the small circular embroidered box, are particularly suitable for beginners and children, and would make an attractive personal gift for a favourite Aunt or Grandma. The covered tissue boxes are not only practical but very attractive. They would be ideal as gifts or for a guest room as the colours can be easily changed from those shown to suit your own decor. The Christmas lanterns are a little more intricate with tops cut to shape so a child would probably need a little help with them, but are such fun, especially as they can be filled with small surprise items.

Quick and simple, these boxes are ideal for children or beginners to make. Choose from the following collection, a selection of which are shown here: the embroidered 'matchbox' (top left), the bold square box (top centre), the mansize tissue box cover (centre), and the small circular embroidered box (bottom right)

Tissue Box Covers

These covers make an everyday item into something which is both colourful and attractive. The design is taken from an eighteenth-century Persian embroidery. They are worked in tent stitch on 10-count plastic canvas in Paterna stranded wool. The boutique and mansize covers fit most brands of tissue. The middle size varies considerably between brands, so it is important to decide which one you are likely to use and make the cover accordingly. The amount of yarn needed will vary if the size is changed. The covers have no base, they simply slip over the box of tissues.

MATERIALS

Plastic canvas: 10-count, one sheet 10½ x 13½in (267 x 343mm) for the boutique size and two sheets for the middle and mansize

Paterna stranded wool, 8 metre skeins

Boutique and middle size: five charcoal 200, seven cream 263, two light pink 906, two dark pink 904, one light mauve 313, one dark mauve 312, one light green 604, two dark green 602, two slate blue 534, one yellow-green 634, one yellow 744

Mansize: six charcoal 200, nine cream 263, two light pink 906, two dark pink 904, two light mauve 313, two dark mauve 312, one light green 604, two dark green 602, one slate blue 534, one yellow-green 634, one yellow 744

PREPARATION

Cutting the plastic canvas

Boutique:

Sides: Cut four (53 x 45 bars).

Top: Cut one (45 bars) square.

Middle size:

Sides: Cut two (28 x 101 bars) and two (28 x 51 bars).

Top: Cut one (51 x 101 bars).

Mansize:

Sides: Cut two (21 x 123 bars) and two (21 x 65 bars).

Top: Cut one (65 x 123) bars.

WORKING THE EMBROIDERY

Use two strands of wool and work in tent stitch following the charts. Work one top and four sides, two long and two short, for each box.

STITCHING UP THE BOXES

Use a single strand of the charcoal wool.

1   Very carefully cut out the central uncovered area, taking care to leave one bar beside the embroidery. Edge stitch all round the aperture.

2   Lie the upper edge of one side against the top, right sides outside, edges matched, and edge stitch to join. Repeat with the other three sides. Join the corners and edge stitch round the lower edge (fig 1).

Boutique (top) and middle size (bottom) tissue box covers

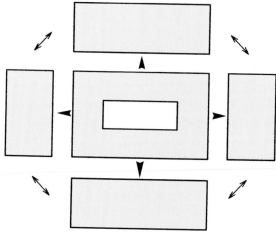

1 Stitching up a tissue box covers

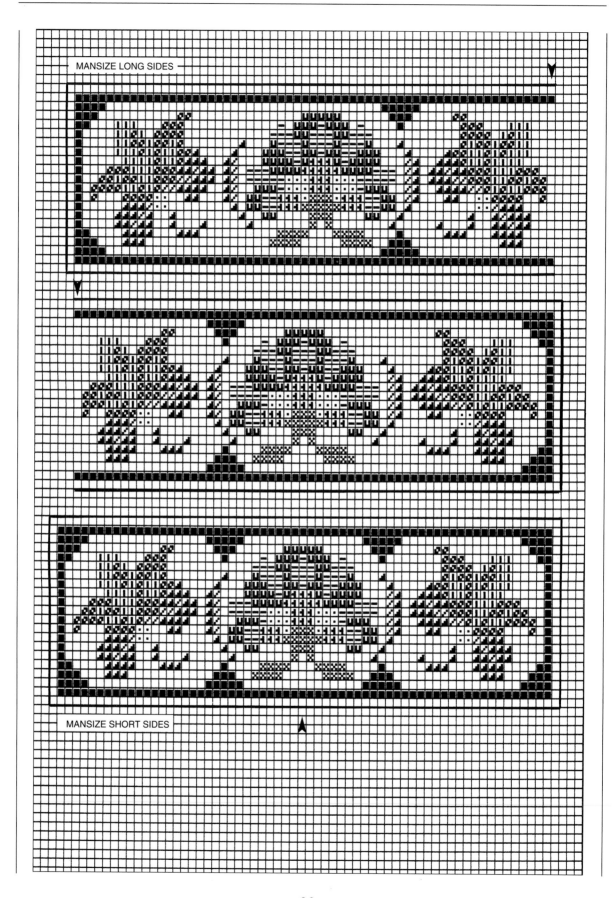

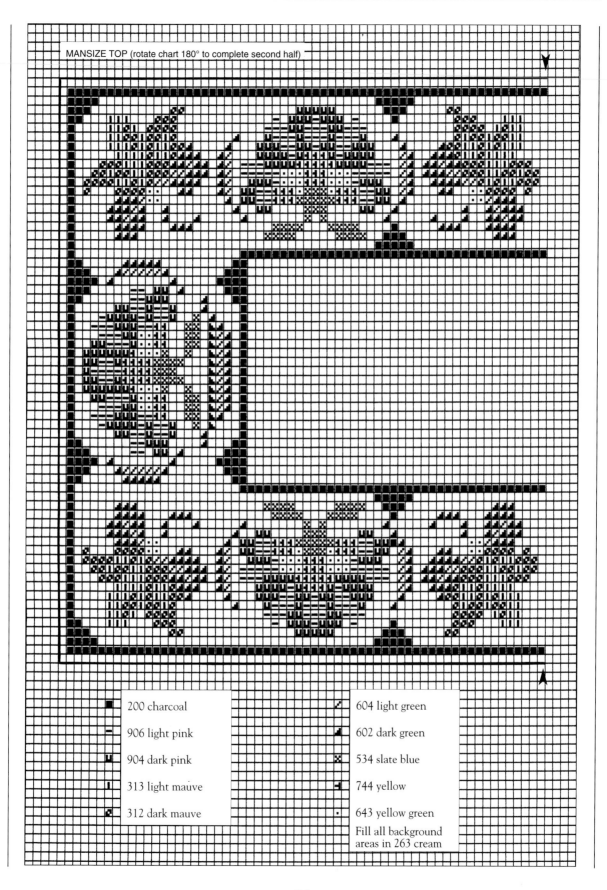

MANSIZE TOP (rotate chart 180° to complete second half)

■	200 charcoal	
=	906 light pink	
U	904 dark pink	
I	313 light mauve	
▨	312 dark mauve	

◿	604 light green	
◢	602 dark green	
▨	534 slate blue	
◣	744 yellow	
·	643 yellow green	
	Fill all background areas in 263 cream	

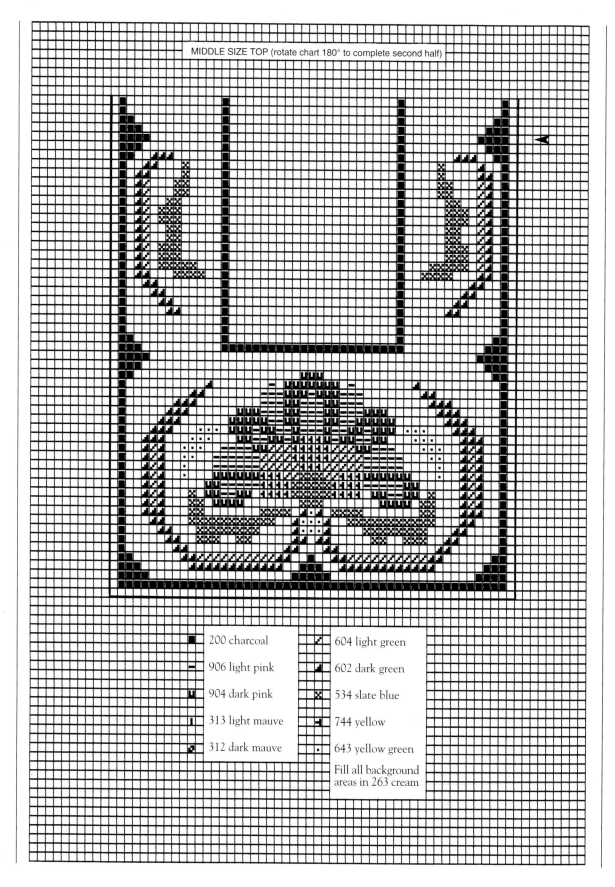

MIDDLE SIZE TOP (rotate chart 180° to complete second half)

■	200 charcoal		◪	604 light green
═	906 light pink		◢	602 dark green
U	904 dark pink		✕	534 slate blue
▮	313 light mauve		◪	744 yellow
◪	312 dark mauve		•	643 yellow green

Fill all background areas in 263 cream

MIDDLE SIZE LONG SIDES

MIDDLE SIZE SHORT SIDES

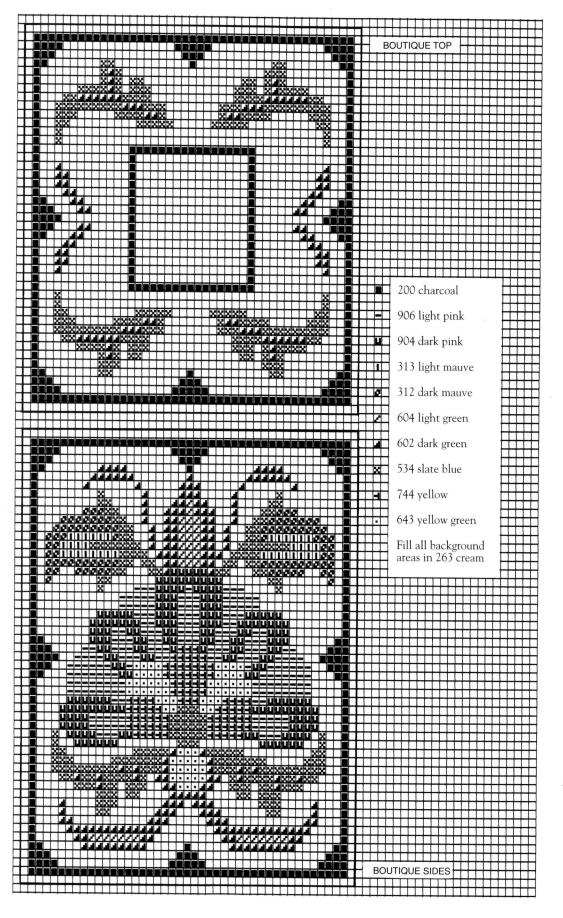

BOUTIQUE TOP

■ 200 charcoal

= 906 light pink

Ш 904 dark pink

I 313 light mauve

⊠ 312 dark mauve

∕ 604 light green

− 602 dark green

⊠ 534 slate blue

⊣ 744 yellow

. 643 yellow green

Fill all background
areas in 263 cream

BOUTIQUE SIDES

Christmas Tree Lanterns

❏

These quaint little lanterns open up and have quite a roomy interior to hold small gifts for the tree. They are quick to work and would make attractive small presents which could then be used again and again for decoration in future years.

MATERIALS

Plastic canvas, standard 7-count, one sheet 10½ x 13½in (267 x 343mm) (enough to make five lanterns, if cut with care)

Paterna stranded wool, 8m skeins – two of main colour (enough for one lantern)

Anchor Pearl cotton, 8m skeins – half a skein yellow 297 (enough for one lantern)

Small curtain ring, preferably metal

Bead for the door knob

Velcro, a small piece of the hook variety

Yellow sewing thread

PREPARATION

(for a single lantern)

Cutting the plastic canvas

Sides: Cut four (11 x 11 bars).

Base: Cut one (11 x 11 bars).

Door: Cut one (9 x 9) bars.

Top: Cut four (11 x 9 bars).

WORKING THE EMBROIDERY

Use the full three strands of wool or three thicknesses of Pearl cotton.

Following the charts work three sides, one door, one base and four top sections.

ASSEMBLING THE LANTERNS

1   Very carefully cut away the inner section of the fourth uncovered side piece (11 x 11 bars) to make the door frame two bars wide. Overcast round three edges of the aperture. Overcast round three sides of the door. Do not fasten off but leave the thread for making the hinge later.

2   Stitch a bead door knob to the centre of the

edge opposite the hinge and a small piece of Velcro behind it on the wrong side.

3   Lie the uncovered edge against one uncovered edge of the aperture and overcast to join the door to the frame (fig 2a).

4   Very carefully cut away the uncovered mesh on each top section, taking care to leave one bar

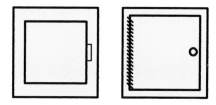

2a Stitching on the door

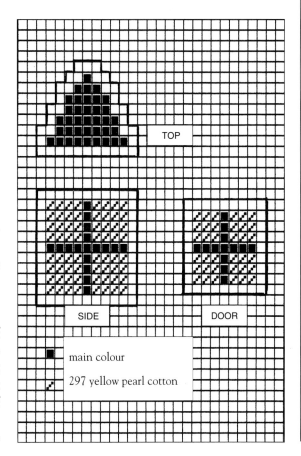

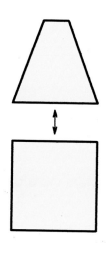

2b Stitching the side to the top

beside the embroidery. Overcast the sloping edges in the main colour.

5   Lie the lower edge of a top section against the top uncovered edge of the door frame, right sides outside, and overcast to join. Repeat with the other three sides (fig 2b).

6   Lie the lower edge of one lantern lower side against the base, right sides outside, and overcast to join. Repeat with the other three sides (fig 2c).

7   Overcast the corners of the sides to join them. Using a single strand of wool overcast the sloping edges to join them. There will be a small square gap at the top.

8   Finally, stitch the ring to the top of the lantern. If you wish the lanterns may be sprayed with fake 'snow' to give a Christmassy effect.

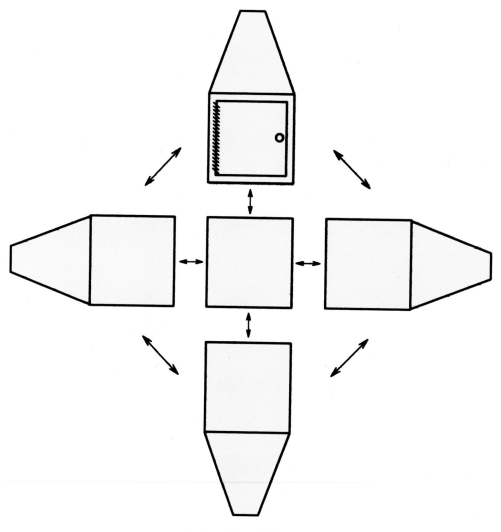

2c Assembling the lantern

Bold Square Box

❏

This striking little box has a bold pattern which has been adapted from a carpet design. The inner sides are set in from the edge of the base and the top fits over the whole box, creating good rigidity. Satin stitch has been used for the inner sides giving a neat finish so a lining is not necessary.

MATERIALS

Plastic canvas, ultra-stiff 7-count, one sheet 12 x 18in (305 x 457mm)

Paterna stranded wool, 8m skeins – four dark blue 510, two cream 263, one light blue 511

Anchor Pearl cotton 8m skeins – two dark pink 76, one light pink 75

PREPARATION

Cutting the plastic canvas

Box top and base: Cut two (30 bars) square.
Box sides: Cut four (14 x 30 bars).
Inner box sides: Cut four (13 x 28 bars).

WORKING THE EMBROIDERY

1 The embroidery uses two strands of the Paterna wool and the Pearl cotton doubled. Work the top, base and four sides following the charts, noting that the two outer bars of the base are left uncovered at this stage.

2 Cover the four inner sides with lines of alternating satin stitch.

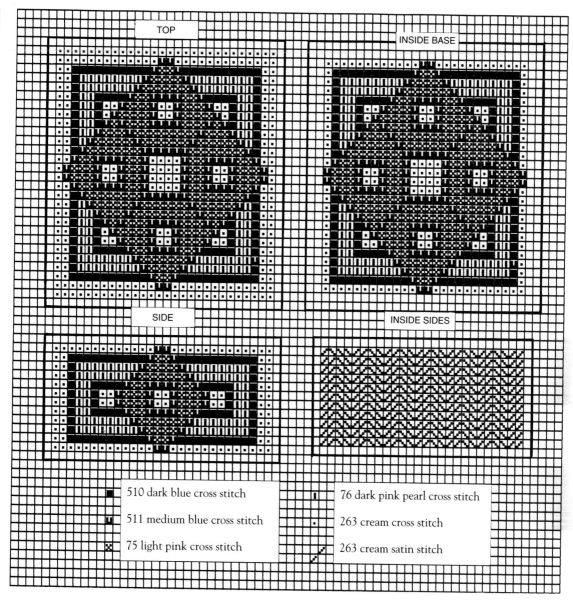

■	510 dark blue cross stitch
∪	511 medium blue cross stitch
⊠	75 light pink cross stitch

I	76 dark pink pearl cross stitch
.	263 cream cross stitch
╱	263 cream satin stitch

MAKING UP THE BOX

1 With the box base right side up, lie one inner side over it, also right side up, with one long edge along the bar next to the edge. Join by overcasting (fig 3a). Repeat for the other three sides.

2 Join the corners by overcasting, then edge stitch round the upper edge and the base (fig 3b).

3 Lie one lid side against the lid top, wrong sides facing and edges matched up, then edge stitch to join. Repeat with the other three sides.

4 To complete, edge stitch to join the corners, then edge stitch all round the uncovered edge and finally slip the lid over the box base.

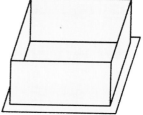

3a Stitching the sides to the base

3b The completed inner box

99

Embroidered 'Matchbox'

❏

Everyone loves a little box and this would be ideal for storing those small treasures which delight children. Being a craftsperson I tend to think of every box in terms of storing sewing things, and this is a good size for holding small scissors, sewing cotton, thimble and spare buttons – just the thing to take on holiday or to give as a Christmas present.

MATERIALS

Plastic canvas, standard 7-count, one sheet 10½ x 13½in (292 x 343mm)

Paterna stranded wool, 8m skeins – three cream 263, one dark green 690 Anchor Pearl cotton, 8m skeins – one green 261, one light peach 08, one dark peach 338

PREPARATION

Cutting the plastic canvas

Outer box top and base: Cut two (20 x 30 bars).

Outer box sides: Cut two (8 x 30 bars).

Drawer base: Cut one (18 x 30 bars).

Drawer sides: Cut two (6 x 18 bars) and two (6 x 30 bars).

WORKING THE EMBROIDERY

1   Use two strands of the Paterna wool and the Pearl cotton doubled. For the outer box work a top, base and two long sides following the charts.

2   For the drawer, cover each section with lines of reversed satin stitch over two bars in the cream wool.

MAKING UP THE BOX

1 To assemble the box, lie one outer box side against the top, right sides outside, edges matched up, and edge stitch to join. Then edge stitch the other side to the opposite edge of the top. Join the second main oblong section to the sides, so forming the open-ended box (fig 4a).

2 Edge stitch around both ends.

3 For neatness make the drawer up with the right sides outside on the two ends and inside on the base and long sides. Lie one short drawer side against the base with edges matched up, wrong

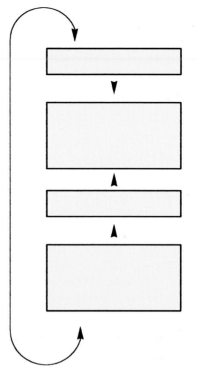

4a Stitching up the outer box

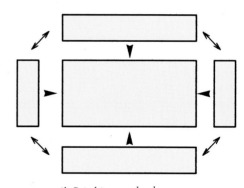

4b Stitching up the drawer

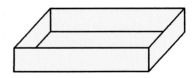

4c The completed drawer

side against right side of base, and overcast to join. Lie a long side against the base, right sides facing, and overcast to join. Repeat with the other two sides (fig 4b).

4 Join the corners and overcast round the upper edge (fig 4c). Then slip the inner box inside the outer cover and your 'matchbox' is complete.

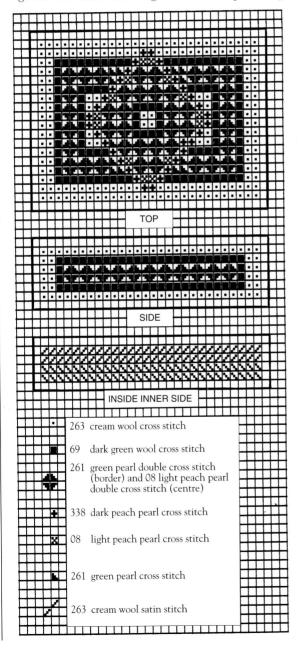

	263	cream wool cross stitch
	69	dark green wool cross stitch
	261	green pearl double cross stitch (border) and 08 light peach pearl double cross stitch (centre)
	338	dark peach pearl cross stitch
	08	light peach pearl cross stitch
	261	green pearl cross stitch
	263	cream wool satin stitch

Small Circular Embroidered Box

❑

The use of textured stitches and varied yarns makes this little box interesting to stitch. The double cross stitch contrasts pleasantly with the tent stitch and the sheen of the Pearl cotton stands out nicely against the wool. The lid has a smaller under-section, which fits inside the box and prevents it slipping off.

MATERIALS

Plastic canvas, standard 7-count, one sheet 10½ x 13½in (267 x 343mm) and three 3in (76mm) diameter circles

(Yarn colours are for the blue version, with yellow alternatives given in brackets)

Paterna stranded wool, 8m skeins – three blue 560 (marigold 800) and one cream 263 (cream 263)

Anchor Pearl cotton No 5, 5gm skeins – one light blue 128 (cream 386) and one dark blue 129 (yellow 306)

PREPARATION

Cutting the plastic canvas

Side: Cut one (12 x 60 bars).

Backing strip: Cut one (12 x 8 bars).

For the lining: Cut one (10 x 58 bars).

For the underlid: Cut one bar off the outer edge of one of the circles.

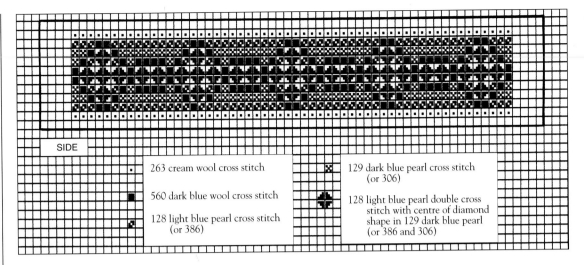

SIDE

·	263 cream wool cross stitch
■	560 dark blue wool cross stitch
◨	128 light blue pearl cross stitch (or 386)

⊠	129 dark blue pearl cross stitch (or 306)
✛	128 light blue pearl double cross stitch with centre of diamond shape in 129 dark blue pearl (or 386 and 306)

WORKING THE EMBROIDERY

Work with two strands of wool and the Pearl cotton doubled.

1 For the box side, tack the backing strip (8 x 12 bars) to the right edge of the mesh (12 x 60 bars) underlapping it by four bars (see page 106/E).

2 Leaving the first and last four bars uncovered work the embroidery from the chart above, the yarns for the yellow version are given in brackets.

3 Lap the left edge over the backing strip on the right, matching up the bars (there will be a small gap between the straight edges) and complete the embroidery through both layers to join into a ring (see page 106/E).

4 To work the base, leave the outer bar uncovered and work a round of satin stitch over the next three bars of one circle followed by another over three bars and one over two bars. As the bars of a circle get fewer towards the centre of a circle the number of holes lessen. Consequently two stitches must be worked into one hole of the inner line as necessary to keep the stitches looking the same. Work a cross stitch over the central intersection.

5 To work the lining, leave the first and last four bars uncovered and work lines of reversed satin stitch over two bars across the lining (10 x 58 bars), alternating the four yarns to give a pleasing effect. With the right side inside lap the left edge over the right, matching up the four uncovered bars and complete the embroidery through both layers to join into a ring. Overcast round both edges in dark wool.

6 To work the lid. Work a round of cross stitch in cream wool over the bar next to the edge followed by one in dark wool. Next work satin stitch over two bars in dark Pearl cotton, a round of cross stitch in dark wool, straight stitch over one bar in light Pearl, and satin stitch over two bars in light Pearl. Work a cross stitch over the central intersection in light Pearl cotton.

7 To work the underlid, work a round of satin stitch over the two bars next to the edge of the trimmed circle in dark wool, followed by a round over three bars in cream wool and one round over two bars in dark wool. Work a cross stitch over the central intersection and overcast round the edge of both circles in dark wool.

MAKING UP THE BOX AND LID

1 Place the base wrong side down with the side over it and edge stitch to join (fig 5a). Edge stitch round the top edge. Slip the lining inside the box.

2 Using a single strand of dark wool slip stitch the underlid invisibly to the centre of the wrong side of the lid, or glue in place (fig 5b).

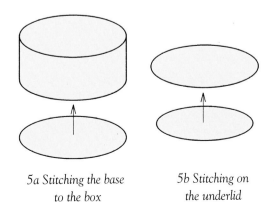

5a Stitching the base to the box   *5b Stitching on the underlid*

103

Basic Techniques

There are some basic techniques which are common to many of the projects. To avoid excessive repetition within the projects themselves, these are described here. It is hoped that this will be useful to you if you wish to design and construct your own boxes, or if you're seeking alternative ways to complete the projects.

A COVERING CIRCULAR CARD WITH FABRIC

1   Card for lining a plastic canvas circle should be cut so that when placed against the mesh the card edge reaches a position between the two outer bars all round, allowing room for the needle to pass through when stitching up.

2   Using the card circle as a guide cut the fabric, allowing extra all round for turning; ⅜in

(16mm) in small boxes, 1¾ih (44mm) in large. From the right side of the fabric run a line of running stitches, about ⅜ to ½in (10 to13mm) from the edge. Do not fasten on and off, leave the ends for pulling up later (fig 1a).

3   Lie the fabric right side down with the card circle centrally over it. Pull up the stitching enclosing the card, tie off with a bow and check for fit (fig 1b). Make any adjustments needed, then tie off securely. Lace across from side to side (fig 1c).

4   If a padded finish is required, wadding the same size as the card may be placed between the card and fabric for lid and base linings.

A quicker method, which is quite satisfactory if the exact size of the circle is known, is to fold the turning over the card and glue in place (fig 1d).

B MOUNTING EMBROIDERY ONTO CIRCULAR CARD

This is mounted over the card as above but should be laced not glued as exact positioning is important.

1   Work the embroidery as directed and press well on the wrong side with an iron over a towel. This can then be mounted over 2mm card to form the lid of the box, as in the large embroidered box, or over 1mm card to be placed behind a frame as in the medium and small embroidered boxes. In the latter cases the card is cut ½in (13mm) larger than the aperture.

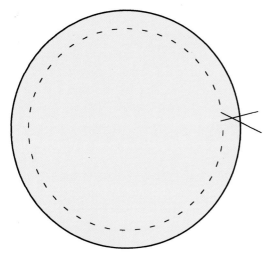

1a Preparing the fabric

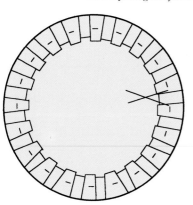

1b Enclosing the card

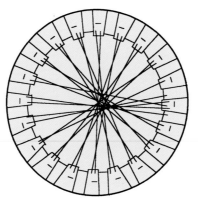

1c Lacing the turnings

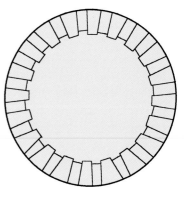

1d Gluing the turnings

2 Trim the embroidered fabric into a circle, allowing ¾ to 1½in (19–38mm) all round for turning. Overcast the edges by machine or hand if the fabric is inclined to fray.

3 Work a line of running stitch all round, about ½in (13mm) from the edge, without fastening on or off, leaving ends for pulling up later.

4 Cut out two, three or four circles of wadding, depending on the effect required. These may all be the size of the card or two the size of the card, one slightly smaller and one slightly smaller still.

5 Lie the embroidery right side down with the wadding centrally over it, the two largest pieces of wadding first and then those in decreasing size. Place the card on top and carefully pull up the running stitch and fasten off with a bow, to allow for any adjustment (fig 2a). Check on the right

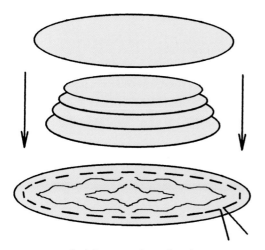

2a Mounting the embroidery

side that the pattern or embroidery is exactly as you want it, making any necessary adjustments. Test on the box for a correct fit – the fabric may be removed and the size of the card altered if necessary. When satisfied tie off the ends securely. Lace across from side to side (fig 2b).

2b Lacing the embroidery

C MOUNTING PATCHWORK ONTO LIDS

Once the patchwork has been prepared (see page 112/K) it is too bulky to be mounted *over* card so it is cut to the same size as the card and mounted *onto* it. For a lid with a side, the card should be covered with fabric. This is not necessary for a lid with a lip as the patchwork is enclosed between two pieces of mesh or card. For further information about the construction of this type of lid see instructions for a lid with a side, pages 106/D for plastic canvas, or 108/H for card and fabric.

LID WITH A PLASTIC CANVAS FRAME

1 Using a card circle as a guide (which must be a little smaller than the lid diameter), trim the patchwork to the same size and overcast the edge.

2 Cut three wadding pieces, one the size of the aperture, one slightly smaller and one smaller still.

3 Lie the card covered side down, with the wadding over it in order of size, smallest first. Spread adhesive round the edge of the card and place the patchwork over it (fig 3). Ease it out round the edges for a firm fit, holding it in place until bonded.

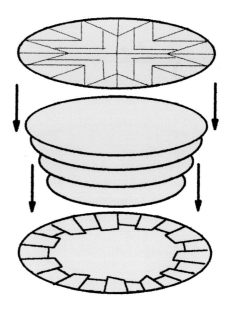

3 Mounting patchwork on to card

LID WITH A FABRIC AND CARD FRAME
Prepare as steps 1 to 3 above, but note that the 1mm card for mounting the patchwork should be about ½in (13mm) larger than the aperture of the lid.

D MAKING LIDS IN PLASTIC CANVAS

To make the basic lid frame, work a border of tent stitch round the lid mesh over the bars next to the edge. Carefully cut out the central uncovered area, leaving one bar inside the tent stitch. Trim off the spikes and overcast or edge stitch the inner edge. Work a line of tent stitch over the bar next to the edge of a second mesh circle for the underlid.

FIT-ON LID WITH LIP

1   To make the lip for a large box you may need to join two pieces of mesh (these will need to be about four bars wide). Overlap the short edges of the two lid lip sections by four bars and tack, creating one long piece. For all sizes of lid, leaving the first and last four bars uncovered, work lines of tent stitch along the lid lip. Overlap the ends, matching up the four bars, and complete the embroidery through both layers, joining into a ring.

2   Place the lid lip centrally over the underlid and overcast to join, taking the stitches over the bar next to the tent stitch. Overcast the uncovered edge of the lip. Place the prepared lid lining card within the lip and slip stitch into place.

3   Place the lid frame and underlid together, right sides outside, and edge stitch halfway round to join. Slip the prepared patchwork or embroidery inside and complete the edge stitching (fig 4).

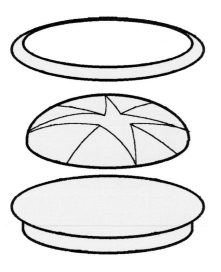

4 Mounting patchwork or embroidery
in a lid with a lip

LID WITH A SIDE

Prepare the lid sides and frame as described in the project, or according to your own design. Edge stitch the frame to the lid side (fig 5). Place the prepared embroidery or patchwork behind the frame (see pages 104–105/B and C) and, using toning sewing thread, slip stitch invisibly in place, taking the stitches over alternate bars of the mesh. If the top is embroidered, cover a circle of card with lining fabric and stitch or glue this in place inside the lid, covering the raw edges.

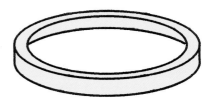

5 A lid with a side

E STITCHING UP A CIRCULAR BOX IN PLASTIC CANVAS

If the side is being embroidered, work this first, leaving the first and last four bars of mesh uncovered. Complete the embroidery after joining the mesh into a ring. If the side is to be covered with fabric this is done after joining into a ring.

LARGE BOXES

If the mesh for the side needs to be joined, as in the box on page 14, cross stitch a backing strip to one end of a side section underlapping it by four bars. Lap one edge of the second piece over the backing strip, matching up the four bars, and stitch in place forming one long length. Then proceed as for the small boxes.

SMALL BOXES

Cross stitch a backing strip securely to the right edge of the side section of mesh, underlapping it

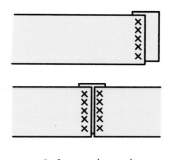

6a Joining the mesh

by four bars and matching up the holes. Lap the left edge over the right edge of the backing strip matching up the four bars and stitch securely in place (fig 6a). There will be a small gap between the straight edges.

FABRIC-COVERED BOXES

1   Place the Vilene around the outside of the box side, mark the overlap, then trim to this line so that the edges will just meet.

2   Lie the patterned fabric for the outside of the box right side down with the Vilene on top, leaving an equal turning allowance at each end and ½in (13mm) along the lower edge. Herringbone all round to hold in place (fig 6b), making tiny stitches on the right side.

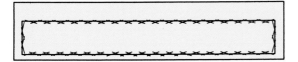

6b Stitching the Vilene in place

3   Join the fabric and Vilene strip into a ring by tacking a seam close to the Vilene using a long machine stitch or close hand tacking. Try it over the box-side ring to test for size, making any necessary adjustment, then stitch the seam securely. Press the seam open with an iron and trim to ¼in (6mm) (fig 6c). Turn through to the right side and fold the lower edge inside over the Vilene and tack.

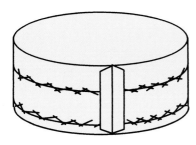

6c Attaching the Vilene

4   Place over the outside of the box with the folded edge of the strip just above the lower edge of the box side, and slip stitch in place taking the stitches over alternate bars of the mesh (fig 6d). Space must be left for the needle to pass through when stitching up. Fold the upper turning to the inside of the mesh and catch in place, taking the stitches through the line of holes next but one to

6d Placing the fabric over the mesh

the edge. Try not to let the stitches show on the outside of the box.

STITCHING UP THE BOX

Stitch a covered card circle to the base, fabric side down. Then place the box side over it and edge stitch or overcast all around to join (fig 6e).

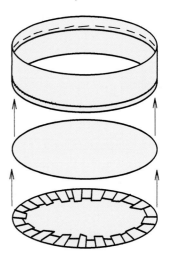

6e Stitching up the box

F   LINING A CIRCULAR PLASTIC CANVAS BOX

1   For a large box overlap the short edges of the two pieces of lining mesh by four bars, cross stitch through both layers to join securely. For all sizes repeat to join into a ring. If wished the ring may be lined with wadding (fig 7a).

2   Stitch a crossway seam in the lining fabric using a long machine stitch or close hand

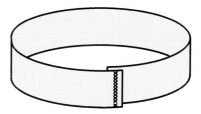

7a Joining the mesh ring

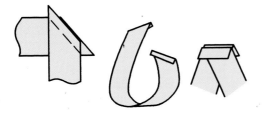

7b Making a crossway join in the lining

tacking (fig 7b). Place inside the mesh ring to test it for size, tacking the turning over one edge. Remove, adjust the seam if necessary and then stitch securely. Place inside the lining mesh, wrong side to the mesh, fold the turnings over the edges and tack along each edge. Lace across to hold them in place, removing the tacking as you do so (fig 7c). Place inside the box. If the box has a lid which fits over a lining the upper turning should be of sufficient depth to conceal the raw edges when the lining is in place.

7c Lacing the lining

G MAKING FIT-ON AND SLIP-IN LIDS IN FABRIC AND CARD

The method is similar for all box shapes, the lining will either be level with the top of the box (a fit-on lid), in which case the lid lining must fit inside it, or it will be lower than the side of the box in which case the lid lining will rest on it (a slip-in lid). If you are following a project these measurements will have been given. Even so, they should be checked carefully as you go along as fabrics differ in thickness. Instructions are given for a circular lid but can be adapted for other shapes.

FIT-ON LID

1   Measure the exterior of the prepared box and cut a circle in 2mm card to this size, or slightly smaller to allow for the thickness of the fabric. Then measure the interior of the box and cut a circle ⅛in (3mm) smaller in 2mm card for the lining.

2   Cover the lid with fabric and wadding as for an embroidered lid (see pages 104–105/B).

3   Cover the lid lining card with fabric. Make sure it will slip into the box easily then ladder stitch or glue to the back of the lid.

SLIP-IN LID

This sort of lid fits inside the box, resting on the lining. Measure the interior of the unlined box and cut a circle in 2mm card a little smaller to allow for the thickness of the fabric. Measure the interior of the box lining and cut a circle in 1mm card ⅛in (3mm) smaller for the lid lining. Proceed as in steps 2 and 3 for a fit-on lid.

H MAKING FABRIC AND CARD LIDS WITH FRAMES

The lid has three layers of card. One layer cut from 1mm or thin card, a little larger than the aperture onto which the embroidery, patchwork or photograph will be mounted. The other two layers are cut from 2mm card to the size of the finished lid. A frame is cut into one of these and the embroidery, patchwork or photograph is sandwiched between the two. Instructions are given for a circular lid but the method is the same or very similar for other shapes.

1   Cut two pieces of wadding for a padded effect, or one of Vilene for a smooth effect, the same size as the lid card circle. Decide the width of the frame and cut out the aperture (fig 8a). Very lightly glue two pieces of wadding together. Then lightly glue one side of the frame and place carefully over the wadding. Allow to bond and then cut the wadding or Vilene out from the aperture.

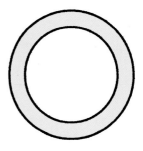

8a Cutting the aperture

2   Cut the frame fabric larger than the card circle by a suitable turning, ⅝in (16mm) for small boxes, 1¾in (44mm) for large. Work a running stitch round the fabric circle from the right side, ¼ to ½in (6–13mm) from the edge,

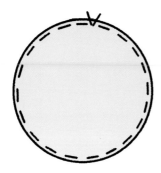

8b Running stitch around the edge

depending on size. Do not fasten on and off, leaving the ends free (fig 8b).

3 Lie, right side down, with the prepared frame centrally over it, wadding side down. Mark edge of aperture on the fabric with a pencil. Remove the frame, and if the fabric is inclined to fray, machine stitch or work small running stitches on the pencil line. Cut out the centre, leaving ⅝in (16mm) for turning inside the line. Snip all round almost to the line at about ½in (13mm) intervals, taking care not to go beyond it (fig 8c).

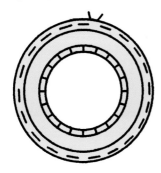

8c Cutting the aperture in the fabric

4 Lie right side down with the frame centrally over it, wadding side down. Spread glue evenly round the aperture – don't go over the edge. Fold

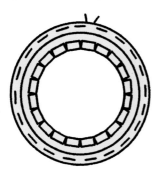

8d Neatening the aperture

the turnings over the card pulling them taut to avoid wrinkles on the right side. You may need to snip a little more to get a good fit. Inspect on the right side an make any necessary adjustment before allowing to bond (fig 8d).

5 Prepare the embroidery or patchwork panel as shown on pages 104–105/B or page 105/C, or use a photograph covered with a piece of acetate for protection. Place a few spots of glue at intervals close to the edge of the embroidery or patchwork. This must not show when the frame is in place. Carefully place the frame over this and allow to bond, having first checked that the position is correct (fig 8e).

6 Place face down and position the second circle of card over it, then pull up the gathering stitches, enclosing both layers. Check on the right side that all is well, then fasten off securely.

7 Cover the card for the lid lining with fabric and ladder stitch or glue to the back of the lid.

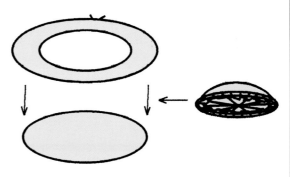

8e Enclosing the panel and backing card

☐ MAKING UP AND LINING A CIRCULAR BOX IN FABRIC AND CARD

MAKING THE BOX

Select the card for the box side and the two circles for the base and lid.

1 For details of joining the card see page 10. Dampen the card for the box side and mould around one of the circles, overlapping as necessary and clip the join together. Push the circle in so that it is about 1in (25mm) from the edge. Place the second circle in position near the other edge and clip together, forming a drum. Leave to dry overnight.

2 Mark dotted lines on the card where it overlaps. Unclip the edges and remove the card. Make a halving join and before gluing, double check that the pared away sections will meet up correctly to form a smooth ring. Smooth the cut away surfaces with an emery board if necessary to give a close fit. Glue in place to form a ring. Wrap sellotape round the box side to cover the join. This will give added strength. Check on the outside of the main ring of card that it is completely smooth, removing any bumps with the emery board, as irregularities will show through and mar the finished appearance.

3   Cut two strips of Vilene the diameter of the box by the width, or if a padded finish is required cut two strips of wadding the diameter by the width plus 1in (35mm) extra.

4   If using Vilene lightly glue this to the outside of the box, trimming the ends to give a butt join with no overlap. Fold the fabric for the side, right sides inside, and tack the short edges firmly, taking ½in (12mm) seam allowance. A large machine stitch is ideal, if it is done by hand small secure tacking stitches should be used. Try it round the card – it should be a close fit. Remove and adjust the seam if necessary then stitch to join using a normal machine stitch. If joining by hand, fold the seam allowances to the wrong side and tack. Place together, right sides facing, and overcast with very small secure stitches. Remove the tacking.

If using wadding, glue the outside of the ring very lightly and wrap the wadding round it. Too much adhesive will go through the wadding and spoil the appearance. It will be ½in (12mm) or so wider at each edge. Trim the excess wadding at the short edges to give a butt join, so avoiding bulk (fig 9a). Prepare the fabric as for the Vilene version above.

5   Place the fabric over the box side as gently as possible, avoiding disturbance to the wadding, if used. It should be a smooth but firm fit. Remove and adjust the seam as described in step 4.

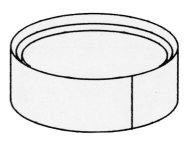

9b Fabric over the wadding

6   Place over the box side (fig 9b). Ease out the wadding if necessary to its original position, being careful to avoid stretching it. There should be an equal amount of excess fabric round each edge. Fold back one edge of the fabric do that it is clear of the card edge and trim the wadding level with the card edge. Repeat for the second edge. Fold the excess fabric to the inside and lace across to hold the turnings in place (fig 9c).

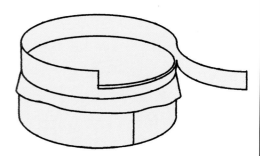

9c Trimming the wadding

7   Cover the base (see page 104/A). Place right side down with the prepared box side over it and tack in place. Using a curved needle and toning sewing thread, ladder stitch to join (see page 124). Remove the tacking (fig 9d).

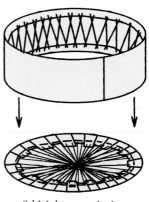

9d Making up the box

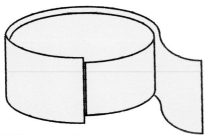

9a Placing wadding over the box side

110

LINING THE BOX

1   Dampen the lining card and place inside the box, pressing out to give a tight fit. Hold in place round the edge with clothes pegs or similar. Leave overnight to dry. Mark dotted lines on the inside against the edges of the overlap. Remove from the box and trim the overlap to ½in (13mm) outside the dotted line. Make a halving join (see page 10) and glue in position, allowing to bond properly before proceeding.

2   Make a crossway join in the strip of lining fabric, taking ½in (13mm) seam, and tacking securely (see fig 7b, page 108). Spread glue sparingly on the inside, place the Vilene or wadding in position and trim the short edges to give a butt join, to avoid bulk. Place the fabric inside the ring, covering the Vilene or wadding, having an equal surplus at each edge. Assess if an adjustment is needed, and then machine or hand stitch. When it is a good fit fold the turnings to the outside and lace across to hold in place. Put the completed side lining into the box. If it is a good tight fit, slip stitching will not be necessary. Remove and attach to the lining base as described below.

COVERING THE BASE

Cover the lining base with wadding, or Vilene and fabric (see page 104/A). Place covered side up and position the prepared side lining over it. Ladder stitch all round to join. Slip the lining into the box.

[J] FITTING A CIRCULAR BOX IN PLASTIC CANVAS

The fittings given here are those which I have found most useful. Variations may be made to suit individual needs, such as a thimble holder in the middle of the upper tray, as in the medium embroidered box (page 28). Standard or soft mesh should be used where it needs to be curved into small circles, to avoid splitting. Embroider the fittings in tent stitch or the same stitch used in making the box. Cut and cover circles as required (see page 104/A).

THE LOWER TRAY

1   Join the mesh side for 6in (152mm) trays with a butted join, as the 121 bars just fits this size circle. For all other sizes joins should be overlapped.

2   Leaving the first and last four bars uncovered, embroider the side mesh for the lower tray. Overlap the left edge over the right and complete the embroidery through both layers, joining into a ring.

3   Using a new circle, or that remaining after the aperture of the lid has been cut, cut a circle with a radius of six bars for a small 4in (102mm) box, nine bars for a medium 6in (152mm) box and nineteen bars for a large 9in (230mm) box. Trim off the spikes. Cut two circles of card, a little smaller than the mesh and cover with lining fabric. Stitch one to the circle for the base of the tray.

4   Place, covered side down, with the prepared side over it and overcast to join (fig 10a). Place the second covered card circle inside. This may be left loose in the base of the box.

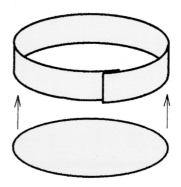

10a Making the lower tray

THE UPPER TRAY

1   Embroider the tray side, and pin box side if you are making a large box, as directed in the project or according to your own design, and join into a ring. Embroider the tray dividers, overcasting each short edge as you do so.

2   For medium and small size boxes, without pin boxes, follow steps 2 to 4. For large boxes see steps 5 and 6. Overcast the long divider to the centre line along the diameter of the remaining trimmed mesh circle. Overcast the shorter divider to the circle, dividing one half into quarters.

3   Slip stitch a covered card circle to the underside of the tray. Place the side over the prepared base and overcast to join. Edge stitch round the top, catching in the top of the dividers

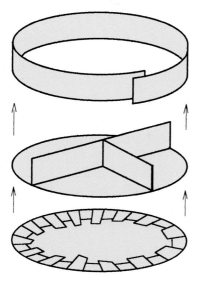

10b Making the upper tray

as you do so. Edge stitch the dividers, taking the stitching through the tray side for extra security.

4 Cut card to fit the tray divisions, cover with patterned fabric and place in the tray (fig 10b).

5 For large boxes, stitch one covered card circle to the mesh circle which has had two bars trimmed from the outer edge. Place this covered side down with the embroidered side over it and overcast to join. Slip stitch the dividers to the pin box, two on opposite sides and one midway between. Slip stitch this centrally to the second covered card circle (fig 10c).

6 Place inside the tray and stitch into place (fig 10d). Edge stitch as in step 3 above.

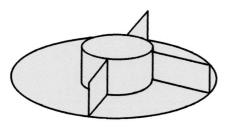

10c The upper tray with a pin box

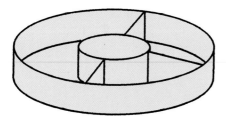

10d The completed tray

K MAKING FOLDED PATCHWORK

Folded patchwork, often called Somerset, folded star or mitred patchwork, is very much easier to work than the appearance suggests. Small strips of fabric, in varying prints and colours, are folded and pressed into triangles which are then arranged in circles from the centre outwards to give a very striking effect. A frame is made, either from embroidered plastic canvas or fabric-covered card, and the patchwork is set behind this to give a decorative lid for a box.

The simple rule to follow when choosing colours is to have dark, medium and light fabrics – a mixture of dark plain, medium patterned and light plain is a good choice. The fabrics used should be of similar weight. Cotton is the usual choice as it presses well. A polyester/cotton mix is also very good, though not quite as easy to press.

Having chosen harmonious colours the key to success is accuracy in pressing and placing the patches. The rest is easy, the sewing being minimal. As the patches are placed in units of four, the fabrics are initially cut into strips which are then cut into four pieces.

PREPARING THE STRIPS OF FABRIC

For a large box, 9in (230mm), cut one 1¾ x 13in (44 x 330mm) strip for every four patches. For a small box, 4 to 6in (102 to 152mm), cut one 1¼ x 10in (32 x 254mm) strip for every four patches.

The standard distance between the points is ½in (13mm) but this may be varied. The red and navy version of the large patchwork box shown on page 20 has the centre and five rows of patches placed ½in (13mm) apart. The light green version of this project has the centre and four rows with patches placed ½ to ¾in (13 to 19mm) apart.

PREPARING THE BACKING

A square measuring the diameter of the circle is needed. This should be white cotton or one of the light colours used in the patchwork. Mark guidelines on the backing fabric with a hard pencil as follows. Fold in half, press and mark the lines across the centre of the fabric in both directions. Repeat, folding from corner to corner for the diagonal lines. For a 9in (230mm) box fold once more to mark sixteen lines in all (fig 11).

PREPARING THE PATCHES

Lie each strip right side down and fold over a small turning of ¼in (6mm) to the wrong side on

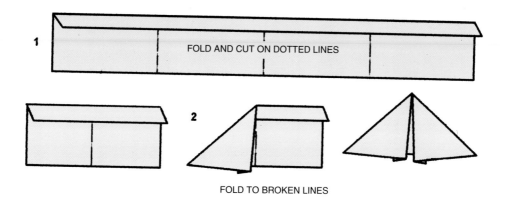

12 *Preparing the patches from the strips of fabric*

one long edge and press. Then fold in half lengthwise and cut, fold again and cut, making four pieces from each strip.

Fold each piece in half, wrong side inside, and press to mark the centre line. Open out and then fold and press down the corners as shown (fig 12), so that the folded edges lie against the foldline. The raw edges when folded down extend beyond the

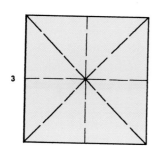

11 *Preparing the backing for a small box (above) and a 9in box (below)*

back layer. This helps to ensure that the raw edges do not show when the patches are positioned. Tack along the lower edge through both layers.

WORKING THE PATCHWORK

As each round is completed, secure round the outer edge with small running stitches. The placement of the colours is a matter of choice. For a small box it is usual to have the patterned fabric in the centre and in round two, with Round 1 in plain fabric, so forming a contrast between them.

Before stitching check on each round that the points of the triangles are correctly placed. In particular, on the final couple of rounds, place the frame over the patchwork and adjust as necessary to ensure that raw edges will not show on completion.

Work the number of rounds needed for the size of the box being made. The following is the placement for the red and navy version of the box on page 14.

Centre – four patterned pieces, placed exactly at the centre of the backing, points meeting and centre and edges matched up with the lines.

Round 1 – eight medium plain pieces, placed in position, opposites first, the points ½in (13mm) from those at the centre.

Round 2 – eight patterned pieces, placed in position as before, opposites first.

Round 3 – sixteen dark plain pieces, placed in position, opposites first, trying the frame in position before stitching.

Round 4 – sixteen light plain pieces, placed in position.

Folded patchwork step-by-step

Round 5 – sixteen patterned pieces, placed and stitched into position. The points may be stitched invisibly if required. Unless the box is to have really hard wear I usually leave mine free as it gives a more three-dimensional effect.

L COVERING RECTANGULAR AND HEXAGONAL CARD WITH FABRIC

Lie the fabric right side down with the wadding centrally over it (if being used). Place the card over this (fig 13a), turn the edges over the card

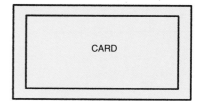

13a Placing the card on the fabric

and lace or glue into position (the lacing method is shown in figs 15a and b on page 115). Smaller sections should be laced in both directions. When covering a long section of card, lace along its length, tucking the short edges under at each end. Gluing is an acceptable alternative to lacing (fig 13b). The section for the lid may have ribbon placed over it or not, as wished (fig 13c).

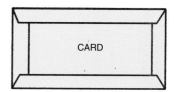

13b Covering the card with fabric

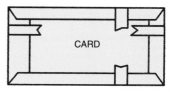

13c Placing the ribbon

In some of the projects covered card is stitched to sections of mesh which have a line of tent stitch worked all round over the bar next to the edge (fig 13d).

13d Fabric-covered card with tent stitch edge

114

M MAKING A MESH LID WITH LIP FOR A RECTANGULAR BOX

1   Place the patterned fabric or embroidery for the lid right side down with three layers of wadding centrally over it, largest first and then in decreasing size. Place the card for the outer lid over this. Fold the turnings over the card and lace or glue in place. Cover the lid lining card with contrast fabric.

2   If using ribbon cut a length of ribbon 2in (50mm) longer than the length of the box. Place in position 1½in (38mm) in from one long edge and stitch or glue the turnings to the back. Cut a piece 2in (50mm) longer than the width and glue similarly in line with one short edge. Tie a neat small bow, trim the ends as necessary stitch and glue over the intersection of the ribbon.

3   Overcast the lid lips to one mesh lid section over the bars inside the tent stitch, joining the corners as you do so. Overcast all round the exposed edge of the lip. Slip stitch the prepared lid lining in place, using the toning sewing thread. It should just fit inside the lip sections (fig 14a). For a lid with sides enclosing thick embroidery, as in the box on page 53, stitch these in place forming a shallow box shape.

4   Carefully cut away the inner uncovered area of the other lid section, to make a frame. Be careful to leave one bar beside the tent stitch. Trim off the spikes and overcast all round the inner edge in the main colour.

5   Place the prepared frame over the underlid and edge stitch round two edges and a little way along the third, to join them. Do not fasten off. Slip the prepared top, right side up, between the two sections and complete the edge stitching (fig 14b).

N MOUNTING EMBROIDERY ONTO RECTANGULAR CARD

1   Check that all thread ends are neatly finished off and press the embroidery from the wrong side. Decide how much fabric you wish to show all round the embroidery as a border, and cut the backing card to this size. If the embroidery is to fit in a frame then the backing card needs to be slightly larger than the aperture. Stretch if necessary (see page 116).

2   Place the embroidery right side down on a work surface, followed by the wadding. Place the backing card centrally on top. Thread a needle with about two yards or metres of strong thread such as crochet cotton. Fold the surplus fabric to the back on the two long edges and lace across to secure them with long herringbone stitches

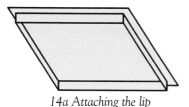

14a Attaching the lip

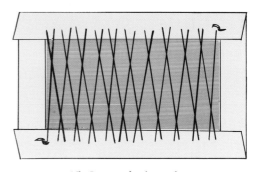

15a Lacing the first side

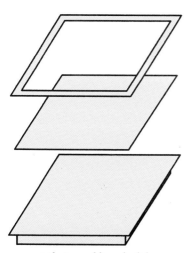

14b Assembling the lid

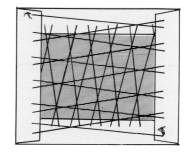

15b Stretching embroidery or fabric over card

(fig 15a). It is important to check on the right side as you proceed that the fabric grain is lying along the edge of the card. When you reach the right edge pull the thread as taut as possible and fasten off very securely. Repeat the lacing process in the other direction, tucking in the corners of the fabric (fig 15b). If the mount is circular work right round (see pages 104–105/B).

STRETCHING CANVAS EMBROIDERY

To stretch your canvas embroidery you will need the following items: a wooden board slightly larger than the embroidery; drawing pins; newspaper; a piece of plain paper the size of the embroidered area.

1   Mark centre lines on the board and the centre of the uncovered edge of the embroidery. Fold the newspaper to be slightly smaller than the finished embroidery and dampen it thoroughly. Place on the centre of the board and cover it with a piece of paper.

2   Place the embroidery centrally over it with the centre lines of the canvas over the centre lines of the board. Pin in position at these four points and, working out from here pin out into a perfect rectangle. You may find it helpful to draw a rectangle on the board, slightly larger than the canvas to act as a guide during pinning.

3   Spray the embroidery to dampen it thoroughly. Leave to dry, preferably in a warm place. This will take about two or three days.

O   STITCHING UP A RECTANGULAR OR SQUARE BOX

FOR A PLASTIC CANVAS BOX

1   Lie one side against the base, right sides outside and edges matched up, and edge stitch to join them. Repeat with the other three sides. Join the corners, then either edge stitch all round the top, or, if the lid is hinged, edge stitch round two short and one long side (fig 16). Edge stitch round three sides of the lid in the same way.

2   Place the uncovered edge of the lid over that of the box and edge stitch to join. Do not work at too tight a tension to allow the box to close properly.

FOR A FABRIC AND CARD BOX

Place the prepared side over the prepared base and ladder or slip stitch together.

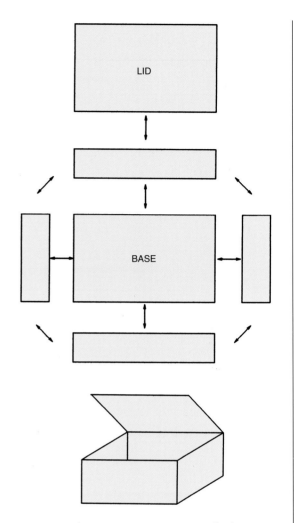

16 Stitching up a square or rectangular box

P   LINING A RECTANGULAR OR SQUARE BOX

The method is the same for a box in plastic canvas or in fabric and card. The depth of the side lining will depend on whether the lid lining is to fit on top of, or inside the side lining.

METHOD 1:   Two sections of lining card are cut to the interior length of the box. The second two side linings will fit between the first (fig 17a) and are cut to the interior width of the box, less the

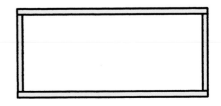

17a Lining a rectangular box

17b Lining a square box

17f Placing the lining of thick card

thickness of the two longer linings, or the pair cut first in the case of a square box (fig 17b). The base lining is cut to the interior measurement inside the side linings. Cover with fabric (see page 114/L). The lining may be glued in place, or ladder stitched. Spread adhesive on the back of the two longer sections, especially along the top edge. Slip into the box and hold in place until bonded. Do the same to the second pair. They fit between the first linings, giving the box rigidity. METHOD 2: The four side sections of card are cut to the interior measurement of the box and the short edges chamfered so that they fit together.

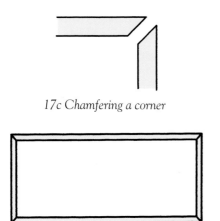

17c Chamfering a corner

17d Lining a box with chamfered corners

To chamfer the edges use sandpaper or a craft knife to cut away the short edge to give a 45 degree angle (fig 17c), then proceed as above (fig 17d). If the lid has been embroidered on plastic

17e Stitching a thin lining to plastic covered lid

canvas a thin piece of covered card just a little smaller than the lid is stitched to the inside of the lid (fig 17e). A second smaller piece of 2mm card is covered and glued centrally to it (fig 17f). This should fit easily into the lined box when closed.

Q MAKING A TRAY IN PLASTIC CANVAS FOR A RECTANGULAR BOX

A tray may rest on card supports placed along the short sides of the box interior or on narrow trays (fig 18a). The placing of the tray dividers is an individual choice. When the tray is in place the right side of the embroidery should be the most conspicuous. Make up the sections so that the right side of the sides face inwards, and the right sides of the larger division face into the centre.

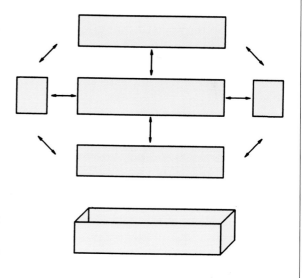

18a Tray support

1 Embroider the sides and dividers, overcasting the short ends of the dividers at the same time.
2 Position the tray dividers according to the suggestions overleaf (figs 18b and c), or according to your own design. Overcast dividers in place, longer ones first.

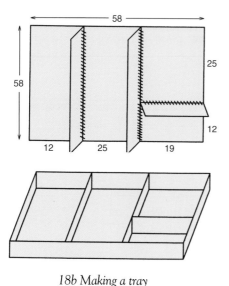

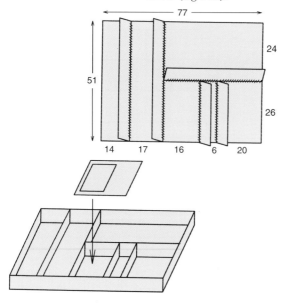

18b Making a tray

3   Cover the thin card for the outer base of the tray and for lining the divisions with contrast fabric.

4   Slip stitch the prepared covered tray base card to the wrong side.

5   Stitch the four sides to the base and join the corners.

6   Overcast all round the top edge, catching in the dividers as you do so. Overcast the top of the dividers. Slip the covered card pieces in place and your tray is complete. The larger tray has a pin box lid which should be overcast to the sections marked with an arrow (fig 18c).

18c Making a large tray

R MAKING HINGES, TABS AND STAYS AND ATTACHING BUTTONS

MAKING A HINGE

Cut fabric twice the width, plus a ½in (12mm) turning allowance, of the finished hinge by 3in (76mm). Fold in half widthways right sides facing and stitch a ¼in (6mm) seam. Press open. Turn to the right side and press with an iron so that the seam lies at the centre of one side (fig 19a).

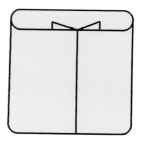

19a Making a hinge

MAKING A TAB

Cut the fabric twice the width of the finished tab, plus ½in (12mm) turning allowance, by twice the length required plus a 1in (25mm) turning. Machine stitch the seam and turn through or fold under and press with an iron ¼in (6mm) on each long edge. Fold the tab in half, right sides outside and oversew along the fold. Fold with the seam down the centre of one side and press again. Fold in half so that the raw edges meet (fig 19b).

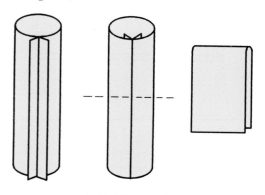

19b Making a tab

MAKING A STAY

Estimate the length required and add 1½in (38mm) extra. Cut two pieces of fabric to this length by twice the finished width plus ½in (13mm) for turnings. Fold under and press ¼in

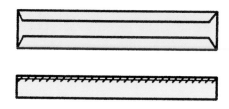

19c Making stays

(6mm) to the wrong side along each long edge. Fold again so that the edges match up and slip stitch invisibly to join (fig 19c).

ATTACHING A BUTTON TO A LID
Cut the card for the lid to the correct size. If it is square or hexagonal draw lines across it from corner to corner to locate the centre. A circle will already be marked at the centre by the compass. Mark two dots ¼in (6mm) apart on each side of the centre and use a stiletto or compass point to make holes on these. When the lid card is covered, using a strong thread take the needle through one hole and out at the centre of the lid. Thread on the button and take the needle to the back through the second hole, then tie off securely (fig 19d).

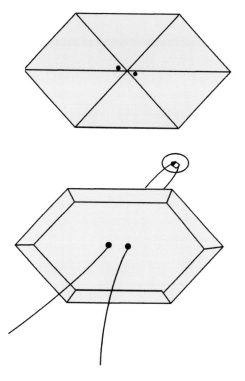

19d Stitching on a button

S MAKING NEEDLECASES

The following instructions give details on making a fabric-covered needlecase such as that shown on page 41, and an embroidered needlecase such as that shown on pages 50 and 51.

MAKING A FABRIC-COVERED NEEDLECASE
Materials given are for making each needlecase. If you are making one to match a box the amounts are included with the box materials.

Materials
7-count plastic canvas, two pieces (24 x 18 bars) and one piece (24 x 3 bars)
Patterned fabric, one piece 4 x 6in (102 x 152mm)
Lining fabric, one piece 4 x 6in (102 x 152mm)
Aida or flannel for a 'page', one piece 3 x 5in (76 x 127mm)
Anchor Pearl cotton No 5, 5gm skein – one each of main colour and contrast
Craft Vilene or thin card, 3 x 9in (76 x 230mm)
2oz wadding, 3 x 9in (76 x 230mm)
Sewing thread to tone with the fabric

MAKING UP THE NEEDLECASE
1 Work a line of tent stitch over the bar next to the edge of the two covers in contrast Pearl cotton then work a line of tent stitch down the spine.
2 Cut two pieces of Vilene or thin card and two of wadding 2⅛ x 3in (54 x 76mm) and two more of Vilene, 2¼ x 3⅛in (57 x 79mm). Using the larger Vilene as a guide and allowing ⅜in (10mm) all round for turning, cut two pieces of patterned fabric and two linings. Lie the patterned fabric right side down with the smaller piece of wadding centrally over it followed by the Vilene. Fold the turnings over the edge and tack, trimming the corners as you go. Repeat with the second piece. Lie on the right side of the mesh and slip stitch in place inside the tent stitch. Prepare the linings in the same way, omitting the wadding and slip stitch to the wrong side of each cover (fig 20a).

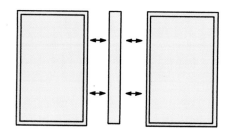

20a Assembling the needlecase

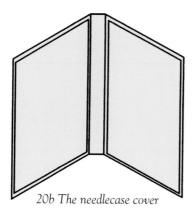

20b The needlecase cover

3 Edge stitch the covers to the spine and then edge stitch all round in main colour (fig 20b).

4 Finish the edges of the 'page' by working a line of herringbone or cross stitch all round the outer edge, ⅜in (10mm) in from the edge using doubled sewing cotton. Turn the fabric over and work a second line on the reverse, over the first

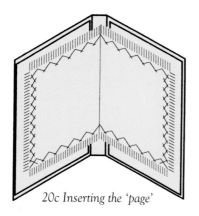

20c Inserting the 'page'

one. This gives a neat decorative edge on both sides. Start and finish the stitching on the reverse side at the centre fold line, where it will show least. Fray out the fabric almost to the stitching.

5 Finger mark the central fold, place over the inside of the cover, and stitch in place along the centre of the spine (fig 20c).

MAKING AN EMBROIDERED NEEDLECASE

This matches the Rhodes Stitch boxes on pages 47 to 53.

Material

Plastic canvas, 7-count, two (28 x 20 bars) and one (28 x 3) for the large size or two (19 bars) square and one (19 x 3 bars) for the small

Lining fabric, one piece 5 x 7in (127 x 178mm) for the large size or 3½ x 6¼in (89 x 158mm) for the small

Craft Vilene, 4 x 6in (102 x 152mm) for the large size or 2½ x 5½in (65 x 40mm) for the small

Aida or flannel for a 'page', one piece 3¾ x 5½in (95 x 140mm) for the large size or 2½ x 4¾in (64 x 121mm) for the small

Paterna stranded wool, 8m skeins – one each of main colour, light main colour and cream

Anchor Pearl cotton, 8m skeins – one main colour

MAKING UP THE NEEDLECASE

1 Work the embroidery from the charts shown below using leftover yarn to match your box.

2 Cut two pieces of Vilene slightly smaller than the covers. The edge should be against the edge stitch. Cover the Vilene with the lining

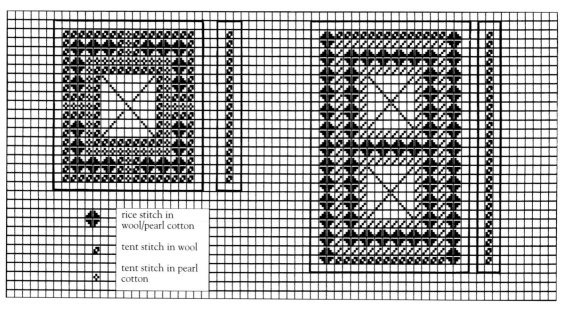

rice stitch in wool/pearl cotton

tent stitch in wool

tent stitch in pearl cotton

fabric and slip stitch to the back of each cover.

3   Edge stitch the sides to the spine and then edge stitch all round.

4   Make and insert the 'page' as for the fabric-covered needlecase steps 4 and 5.

T   MAKING CORDS AND TASSELS

MAKING A CORD

Success in making an even and tightly twisted cord depends on keeping it taut at all times. The following instructions apply to making cord from No 5 Pearl cotton, giving a finished length of approximately 24in (610mm). A pen with a clip is needed for weighting the cord.

1   Cut a length of Pearl cotton 8yd/m long. Fold in half and in half again and knot the ends together.

2   Hold the knotted end and place the looped end over a hook or small door handle. Slip the pen into the loop and hold it so that the yarn is taut. Turn the pen in a circular motion until the cord is tightly twisted, using a finger to push the twists up towards the loop.

3   When really tight substitute your finger for the pen. Place a finger halfway along the cord and keeping it taut, take the knotted end to the hook . Hold both ends together and remove from the hook. Clip the pen onto the looped end to act as a weight. Holding the knotted end up and the pen end down, still taut, let go of the pen and the cord will twist gently until it stops. Withdraw the pen and knot the ends (fig 21a).

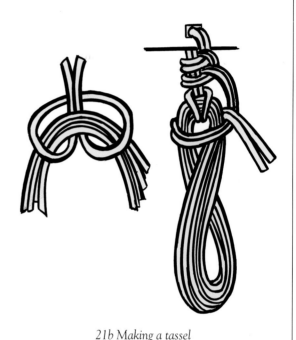

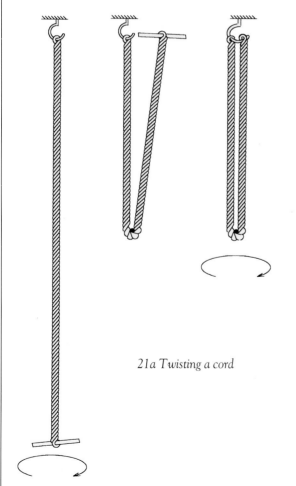

21a Twisting a cord

21b Making a tassel

MAKING A TASSEL

1   Wind some Pearl cotton around three fingers about fifteen times. Slip the loops off. This will now be referred to as the tassel.

2   Take a length of Pearl cotton, about 18in (457mm) long, double it and slip the folded end through the tassel. Take the ends through the loop and pull tight.

3   Thread both ends into a tapestry needle and stitch to the centre opening side of the lid.

4   Wrap the thread around the tassel, about ¼in (6mm) down, and make a knot or two to secure the head. Take the ends down through the centre of the tassel and let them join the loop on the back (fig 21b).

5   Cut the loop and trim the ends.

The Stitches

STARTING AND FINISHING

To start, knot the end of the thread and take it through to the back of the work, 1in (25mm) or so forward from where you are intending to stitch. The stitches cover the thread on the back and the knot should be cut off when reached. After the first row the thread may be joined on by running through the back of previous stitching. To finish off, run the thread through the back of the last few stitches.

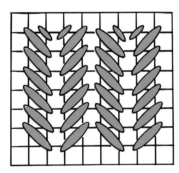

Starting and finishing

ALTERNATING SATIN STITCH

A line of sloping stitches is worked over two threads or bars. The slope of the stitches on the next line is reversed.

Alternating satin stitch

DOUBLE CROSS STITCH

A diagonal cross stitch is worked first over two threads or bars and then straight cross stitch is

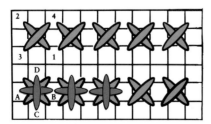

Double cross stitch

worked over it, either in the same yarn or in a contrast. Wool and Pearl cotton make a good combination. This stitch is quicker to work than rice stitch and may be used instead if preferred.

EDGE STITCH *(for plastic canvas)*

Used for joining sections together, or for covering an edge. It has an interesting plaited effect, which shows best if worked from the wrong side. Use a long length of yarn and work at a tight tension, except when joining a lid to a box. Although this stitch may look complicated it is actually just two movements – forward three and back two, repeated. Extra stitches are needed at the beginning and end to fill in properly.

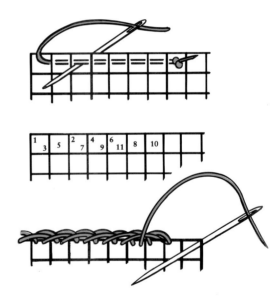

Edge stitch for plastic canvas

1   Bring the needle up in the first hole, take it over the edge and come out at 2, two bars forward (see diagram).
2   Take it back over the edge and out two bars back, in the first hole again.
3   Take it over the edge and out three bars forward.
4   Take it over the edge and out two bars back.
5   Repeat 3 and 4 along the edge until the needle comes up in the last hole. Take it back

over the edge and out one bar back, and bring it up in the last hole again. Fasten off securely.

When turning a corner work three stitches into the corner hole, and continue along the next side.

EDGE STITCH (for cotton canvas)

This is worked in a similar way to that on plastic canvas, this time going forward six threads and back four all along the edge. Fold the turning to the wrong side between the first and second threads next to the embroidery. One thread should show on the right side and the holes should match up.

1 Bring the needle up in the first hole, take it over the edge and come out two threads forward.

2 Take it back over the edge and out in the first hole again.

3 Take it over the edge and out four threads forward.

4 Take it over the edge and out in the first hole again. Continue as follows.

5 Take the needle over the edge and out six threads forward.

6 Take it over the edge and out four threads back.

7 Repeat steps 5 and 6 until the needle comes up in the corner hole. Next, go back four threads and up in the corner hole, back two threads and up in the corner hole again. Work three stitches into the corner hole and continue as before.

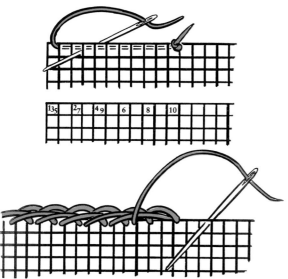

Edge stitch for cotton canvas

FREELY WORKED EYELET

This is a surface embroidery stitch where straight stitches are worked into a central hole and pulled so that a hole forms at the centre. More stitches may then be worked over these, filling up the hole and forming a chunky stitch. The tones of yarn used may be varied in the same stitch.

Freely worked eyelet

FRENCH KNOT

If worked correctly a pretty rose-bud shape is achieved with this surface embroidery stitch. The secret of success lies in keeping the thread taut against the fabric when pulling it through to the back. The full six strands of thread should be used and wrapped round the needle once when embroidering on heavy fabric. When working on finer fabric use less strands.

Bring the needle up to the right side at the position required and hold the thread in your left hand close to the fabric. Wrap the needle round it twice, and keeping the thread taut, insert the point into the fabric close to where it came out. Slide the knot down against the fabric, hold it under your thumb and feed the thread through, only taking your thumb away at the last moment.

French knot

HALF CROSS STITCH

This looks like tent stitch on the right side but has a small straight stitch on the back of the work. It does not cover the fabric as well as tent stitch and is not as hard wearing; however, it takes less yarn and does not distort the canvas as tent stitch does. Start by working from left to right.

Half cross stitch

HERRINGBONE STITCH

As a surface embroidery stitch this is worked moving from left to right between parallel lines, taking a small back stitch alternately on each one. It is also used for lacing two turnings together when lining a box or mounting an embroidery.

Herringbone or lacing stitch

LADDER STITCH

This stitch is worked from the right side and is used for joining sections invisibly when making fabric and card boxes. The needle takes a small stitch in the fold on alternate sides, passing straight across between the stitches. On the hard edge of fabric-covered card the stitch may be at a slight angle for extra strength. Use a curved needle for best results.

Ladder stitch

LARGE DIAGONAL STITCH

Start at the top left-hand corner and work diagonally down taking the stitches over two, three and four bars or threads. Repeat this until you reach the lower edge. At the start of the next row in-filling stitches are needed at the edge of the row you have just worked, and then the stitching repeats itself again. The stitch over two bars or threads being in line with the one over four of the previous row, and the stitches over three bars meeting up.

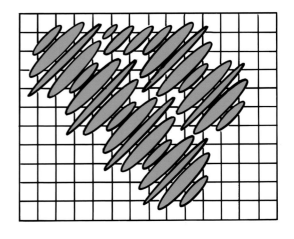

Large diagonal stitch

LARGE DOUBLE CROSS STITCH

A large diagonal cross stitch is worked over four bars or threads with a straight cross stitch over two bars worked over it, either in the same yarn or a contrasting one. The spaces between are filled with straight cross stitch, in the same yarn or a contrast. The spaces at the edge are filled in with tent stitch.

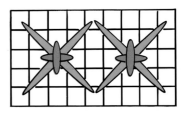

Large double cross stitch

LONG CROSS STITCH

This is worked across one bar and up over two on alternate intersections of mesh. The stitches of the next row fit in between those of the first in a brick effect. Small in-filling stitches are necessary at the edge. It may be worked diagonally up and down for the required number of stitches as shown in the diagram below.

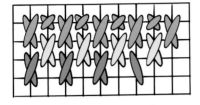

Long cross stitch

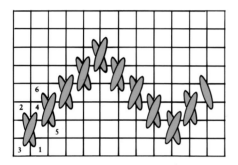

Long cross stitch worked diagonally

LONG AND SHORT STITCH

This is a surface embroidery stitch with only the first row worked in long and short stitch. Subsequent rows are, in theory, worked in the same length, fitting between the stitches of the first row. Because the areas being filled are small and uneven in shape, the stitches should be varied in length to fill the space. The tones and colours may be varied to shade the work, going from light to dark or the reverse.

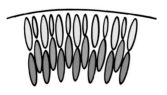

Long and short stitch

OVERCAST STITCH

This is easier to work than edge stitch and may be used instead if you prefer. It requires a thicker thread than edge stitch – three strands of wool or Pearl cotton are ideal on 7-count mesh. Start by bringing the needle up in the first hole, take it over the edge of the mesh or fabric and out in the second hole. Continue like this along the edge, working a stitch into every hole (or at regular intervals if working on fabric), and bringing the needle through from the back to the front each time.

Overcast stitch

RHODES STITCH

This is usually a square stitch worked over an even number of bars or threads, from four upwards. It may also be rectangular, diamond shaped or circular – the method is the same whatever the size and shape. For a square stitch start off with a long sloping stitch, coming up in the lower left-hand corner and going down in the top right. Subsequent stitches come up one thread to the right and go down one thread to the left. On completion the threads should be tied down with a small straight stitch across the centre where they intersect. This may be omitted if the stitch is only four threads square.

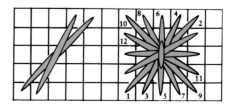

Rhodes stitch

RICE STITCH

A cross stitch over two threads or bars is worked first and then sloping stitches are worked over each corner, usually in a contrasting yarn.

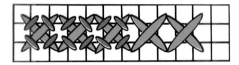

Rice stitch

SATIN STITCH

This surface embroidery stitch is useful for filling small shapes. Work straight stitches closely together across the shape to be filled, keeping a neat edge.

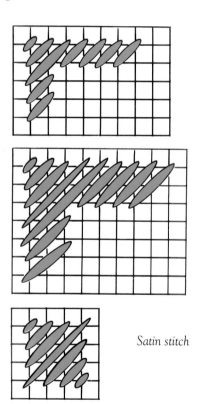

Satin stitch

SMALL CROSS STITCH

This is worked over one intersection of the canvas.

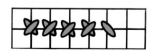

Small cross stitch

STEM STITCH

This is a surface embroidery stitch worked from left to right. Bring the needle up at the beginning of the line to be covered. Take it down to the right and up again a little to the left, keeping the thread below the needle. The lengths of the stitches may be varied, as may the slant. Lines of stem stitch worked side by side make a good filling, as a change from long and short stitch.

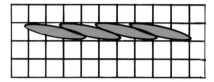

Stem stitch

TENT STITCH

This stitch passes over one intersection of the canvas and should be worked to give a long sloping stitch on the back, as this gives a good cover. Work from right to left on the first row. Subsequent rows may be worked from left to right, but take care the back looks the same. This stitch tends to distort cotton canvas. When stitching on a plastic canvas circle, as the number of holes decreases towards the centre, it is necessary to work two stitches into one hole on the inner line to keep them looking the same on the right side.

Tent stitch

TIED CROSS STITCH

A long cross stitch is worked up over four threads or bars and across two and a straight stitch over two bars is then worked over at the centre.

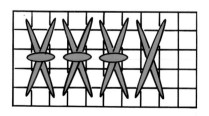

Tied cross stitch

Thread Conversion Chart

Anchor	DMC	Anchor	DMC
8	353	876	503
10	351	880	951
48	963	885	3047
75	3354	894	224
76	3731	895	223
108	211	896	3721
239	702	905	3031
259	772	921	931
261	989	926	822
306	783	939	793
338	921	968	224
373	3045	969	3727
386	746	975	775
387	ecru	976	3325
861	3363	9575	758

Glossary for American Readers

The following list is provided for American readers who may not be familiar with some of the terms used in this book.

UK	USA
clothes peg	clip or spring peg
cotton	floss
craft Vilene	a heavyweight pellon
on the cross	on the bias or diagonal
tacking	basting
wadding	batting
wool	yarn

Useful Addresses

UK

Meg Evans
29 New Road
Welwyn
Hertfordshire Al6 0AQ
(Mail order, for most items listed in the projects)

Shades at Mace and Nairn
89 Crane Street
Salisbury
Wiltshire SP1 2PY
(Mail order, for a range of supplies)

Craft Creations Ltd
Units 1 – 7 Harpers Yard
Ruskin Road
Tottenham
London N17 8NE
(For card and greyboard for lining boxes)

For a list of countrywide shops write to the following:

Coats Patons Crafts
PO Box 1
McMullen Road
Darlington
County Durham DL1 1YQ

DMC Creative World
Pullman Road
Wigston
Leicestershire LE8 2DY

For a list of Paterna stockists write to the following:

The Craft Collection
PO Box 1
Ossett
West Yorkshire WF5 9SA

AUSTRALIA

Coats Patons Crafts
89–91 Peters Avenue
Mulgrave
Victoria 3170

DMC Needlecraft Pty Ltd
PO Box 317
Earlswood
New South Wales 2206

USA

Coats & Clark Inc
30 Patewood Drive
Suite 351
Greenville SC 29615

DMC Corporation
Port Keamy
Building 10
South Keamy
NJ 07032

Martisco Paper Company Inc.
4747 Rte 174
PO Box 198
Marcellus
NY 13108
(For card and greyboard for lining boxes)

for mail order supplies write to the following:

Schrocks Crafts
1527 East Amherst Road
Massillon
Ohio 44646

Needlecraft Shop
103 North Pearl Street
Big Sandy
Texas 75755

Sunshine Crafts
1280 North Missouri Avenue
Largo
Florida 34640

Index